The Incidental Collector

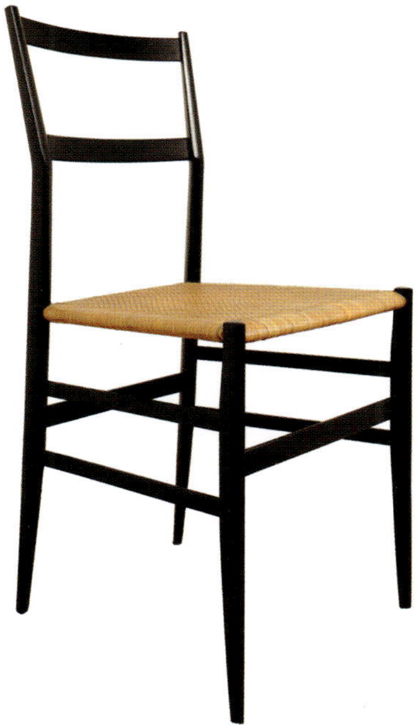

Superleggera chair, Gio Ponti, 1957

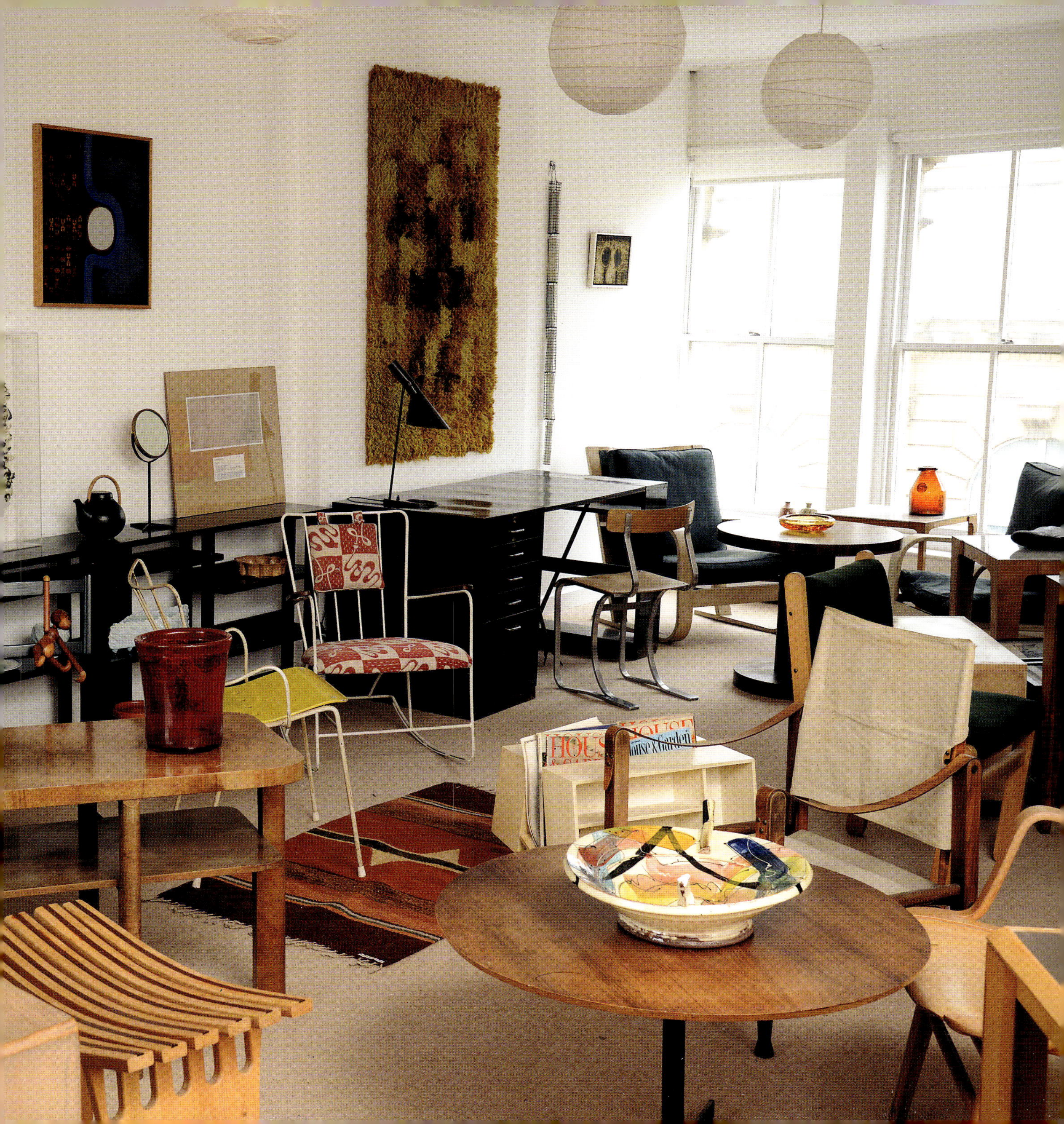

The Incidental Collector

KEN STRADLING AND THE KEN STRADLING COLLECTION

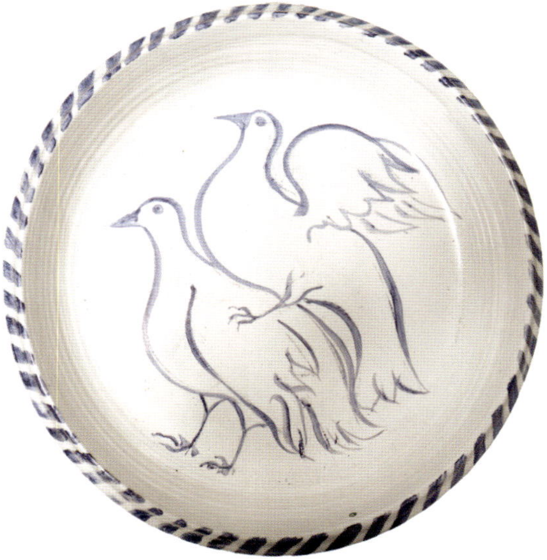

Large bowl, William Newland c.1990

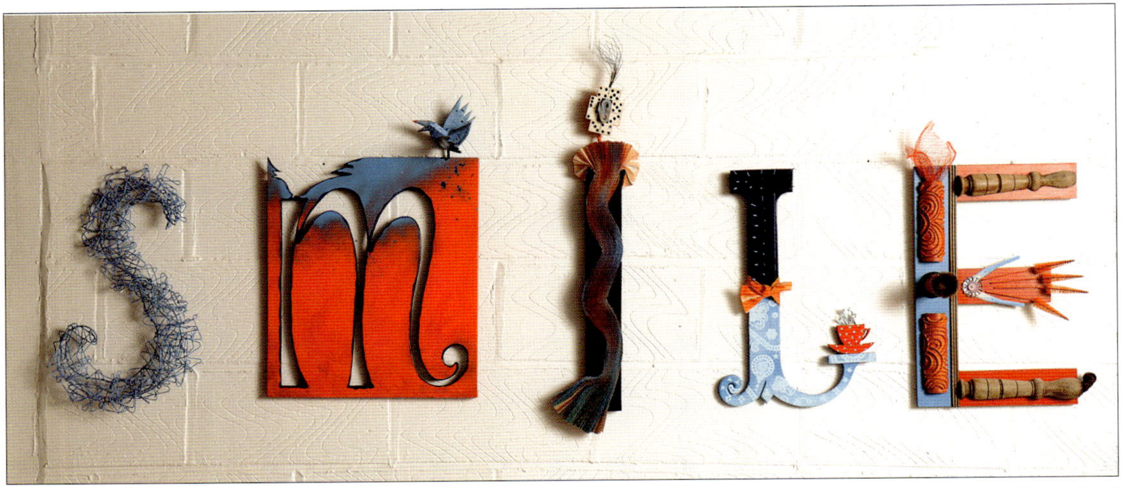

Smile, Eleanor Glover, 2012

The Ken Stradling Collection,
c/o Bristol Guild of Applied Art,
68-70 Park Street,
Bristol, BS1 5JY.
T: 0117 926 5548
E: kscollection@freeuk.com

First published in 2013 by the Ken Stradling Collection
68-70 Park Street Bristol BS1 3JY

ISBN 978-0-9926075-0-0
British Library Cataloguing-in-Publication Data
A catalogue record for this book is available from the British Library

Editors: Oliver Kent and Stephen Morris
The editors would like to thank Chris Yeo and Colin Beales for their help throughout.

Cover design, typesetting and photography by Stephen Morris www.stephen-morris.co.uk
Printed and bound by Jam Jar Bristol

Contents

Foreword 7 Christopher Lloyd
Origins of a Collection: Ken Stradling and Bristol Guild 10 Oliver Kent/Colin Beales/Cleo Witt
'Learning to Look': The Collection in Perspective 20 David Whiting
Buying, selling and collecting post-war glass 33 Graham McLaren
Marcel Breuer and Crofton Gane: The Bauhaus in Bristol 42 Oliver Kent
'A Style To Call Our Own' – The Gane Legacy 43 Max Gane
A Centre for Design Research 48 Oliver Kent/Cleo Witt
Contributors 53
Bibliography 54
Afterword 56 Ken Stradling

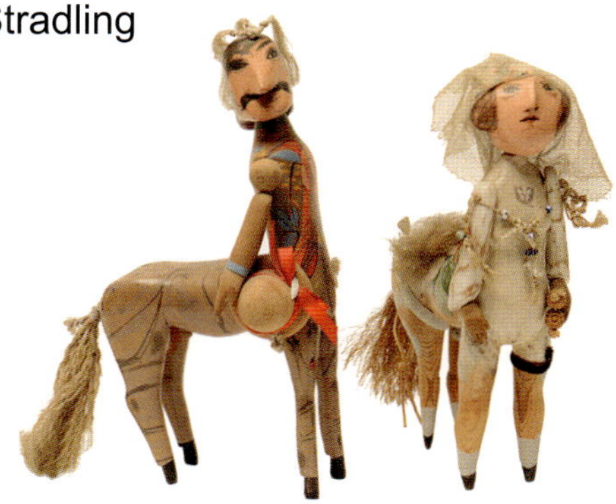

Bride and Groom, Sam Smith 1975

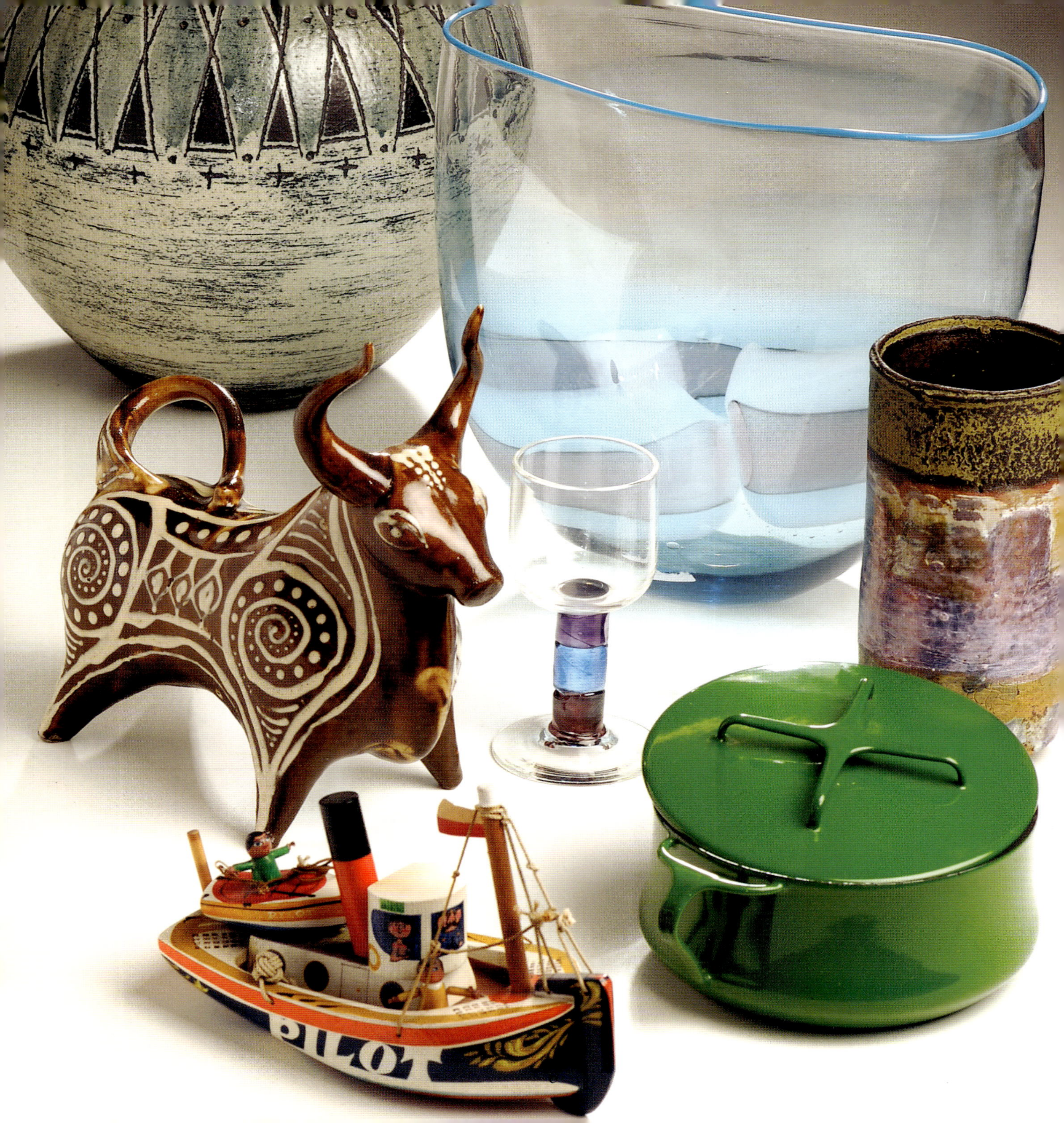
PILOT

Foreword

Christopher Lloyd

There is a moment in the history of any collection when life intersects with art. As far as Ken Stradling is concerned, this is signalled by his distinctive personal appearance. A penchant for fedora hats, buttoned up tieless black shirts and sombre colour coding denote a bohemian air combining undeniable charm with a slightly wicked sense of fun. This fastidious attention to appearance runs counter to the nonchalance that characterises most forms of contemporary dress. One might expect to find such a person portrayed in Sir William Nicholson's much-loved Alphabet of 1897.

Other personal characteristics that contribute to Ken Stradling's success as a collector are his steadfast determination and his saurian alertness. Both are on display when he attends the saleroom. When an item he is interested in obtaining is announced he edges forwards on his seat and rises slowly in order to follow the bidding more closely as the tension mounts. A successful outcome results in a face wreathed in a smile of quiet satisfaction and provides an excuse to celebrate in a carefully chosen restaurant. The calm exterior belies Ken Stradling's enthusiasm for beautiful objects and good living.

In the final analysis, however, what distinguishes a collector is the nature of the collection itself. An innate interest in many aspects of design has led to the wide range of Ken Stradling's collection in terms of materials, techniques and concepts. Over the years he has collected glass, ceramics, pottery, wooden objects and furniture.

Although there is an awareness of historical progression extending back to the 1930s, the collection is more illustrative of contemporary design issues such as the interplay between studio products and industrial output. Ken Stradling was well placed to exploit such juxtapositions as a result of his long association with the Bristol Guild of Applied Art dating back to 1948. Apart from the financial acumen required to make this organisation a business success, it also presented him with many opportunities to travel and to meet artists. Such advantages were eagerly grasped by someone with an open mind, boundless curiosity and, most importantly, a sense of mission.

A significant collection is formed not just because of instinct or courage, but also as a result of discipline and commitment. From an early age Ken Stradling has believed in the fundamental importance of design to the extent that for him it underpins the essential values of our very existence. The emphasis in his collection on everyday objects validates this

◀ A selection of pieces from the Collection including: glass bowl and wine glass, Annette Meech, 1980s | Bull, William Newland 1954 | jar, Robin Welch, c.1985 | Pilot Boat, Sam Smith, 1970s | casserole, Jens Quistgaard, Dansk International, 1954

belief, just as an underlying purpose of the Bristol Guild has been to inculcate an appreciation of the applied arts on a wider social basis – not an easy task in a country that has been slow, if not reluctant, to recognise the benefits of good design. Even though other collectors have shared similar interests and aspirations with Ken Stradling, there remains a pioneering spirit in what he has achieved with comparatively modest means. Only fairly recently has the Victoria and Albert Museum begun to pay serious attention to design dating from after the Second World War and it is surely significant that the Design Museum founded by Sir Terence Conran opened as late as 1989.

A remarkable feature of the Collection is the quiet way in which it sanctifies two fundamental truths. Firstly, modern design is essentially an international movement. Ken Stradling's taste ventures from the Bauhaus furniture of Marcel Breuer, through glass of Scandinavian, Baltic and Italian origins, to Poole Pottery. What is also reflected in the collection is the close inter-relationship between designers on the continent of Europe as a whole thereby undermining any claims of insularity that British artists and critics may harbour. Secondly, there is a quiet confidence and even pride in the skills of British-born artists whose work Ken Stradling has championed often through personal contact.

A long association with the City of Bristol and nearby places such as Bath Academy of Art at Corsham is reason enough for the Ken Stradling Collection to be permanently established at 48 Park Row as a Design Study Centre. More than that, however, is the fact that Ken Stradling's desire to share his love of design and to demonstrate its importance for everyone's well-being will be perpetuated in a place to which he has already contributed so much.

'Ken Stradling is a supporter of a rare kind. Over more than 20 years he has consistently offered invaluble encouragement for my work and social projects. He has taken the risk of buying some of the most interesting, and occasionally the most idiosyncratic work I have made – vital oxygen to go forwards.'
Eleanor Glover

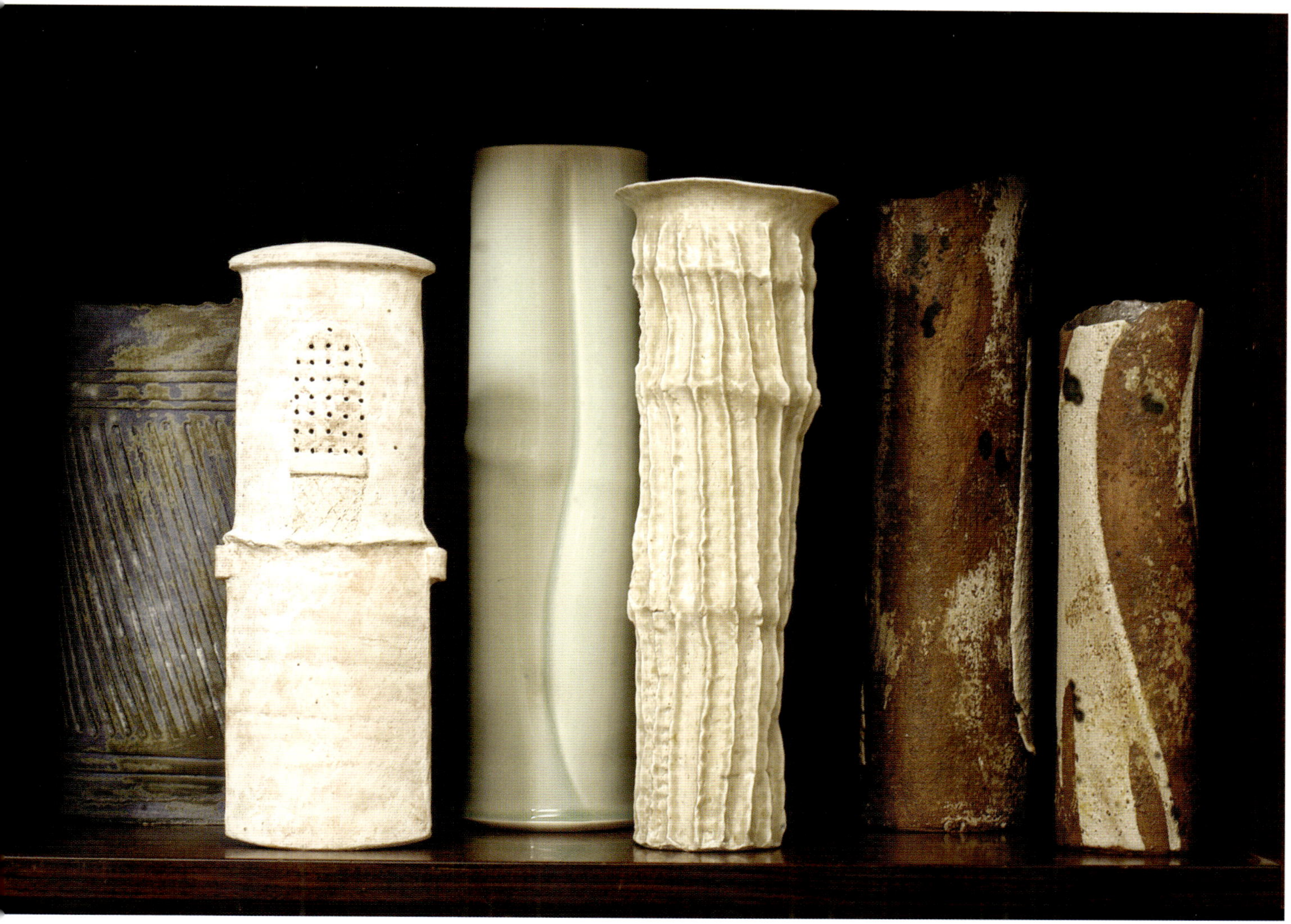

'an attraction to the materiality of objects'

ORIGINS OF A COLLECTION: KEN STRADLING AND BRISTOL GUILD

Oliver Kent / Colin Beales / Cleo Witt

> My critical point is that I'm interested in design generally, whether it's pottery, glass, industrial design or craft and so on, it's all design to me and that's why I can go from one to the other.

The Ken Stradling Collection is a detailed reflection of one man's engagement with design, as a buyer, a retailer, a patron and a collector.

In his role as a buyer, manager and director for Bristol Guild of Applied Art, since 1948 Ken Stradling has been actively involved in the constantly changing world of design and domestic taste. His now superb collection of 20th and 21st-century design began both as a pastime and a necessity – a collation of the buying choices he was making both for Bristol Guild and a newly-acquired family home, and an adjunct to the professional and cultural environment in which he found himself. Buying for retail sale at the Guild often co-incided with his buying for the house in Hotwells that he shared with his wife Betty.

Though sensitive to changing fashions, Ken has always trusted his own interpretation of good taste and quality. Thus the Collection is a very personal view of the world: reflecting Ken's taste in furniture, pottery, glass, fine art and craft objects both handmade and commercial. It is not a formal or didactic account of changing taste and design history, nor is it a history of Bristol Guild.

Ken Stradling was born and brought up in south Bristol. His family, though not affluent, was comfortable and cultivated good taste; Ken's mother would occasionally take him to auctions where he developed an early interest in antiques and connoisseurship, and where he was sometimes allowed to buy things. As a pupil at Bristol Grammar School in the 1930s, Ken's fledgling interest in the arts was cultivated by the headmaster, JE Barton. Barton was a passionate advocate of education in art and design; he wrote for the *Listener* magazine and, as a BBC broadcaster, brought an understanding of art – in particular modernism – to national radio audiences.

Demobbed from the army in 1948, Ken found employment as assistant manager at the Bristol

Bristol Guild: the 'little gift shop' of 1948 is now a thriving but still quirky emporium ▶

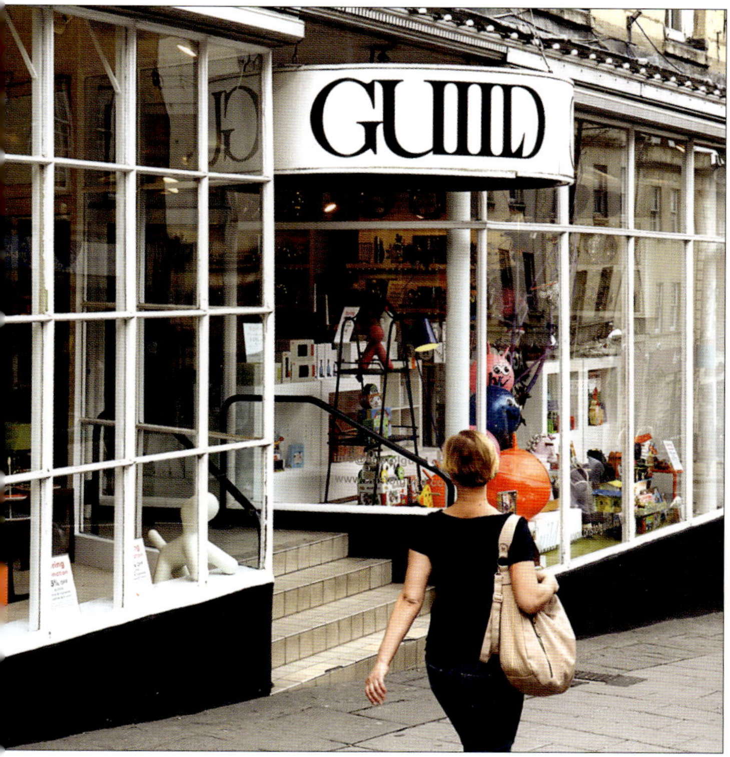
GUILD

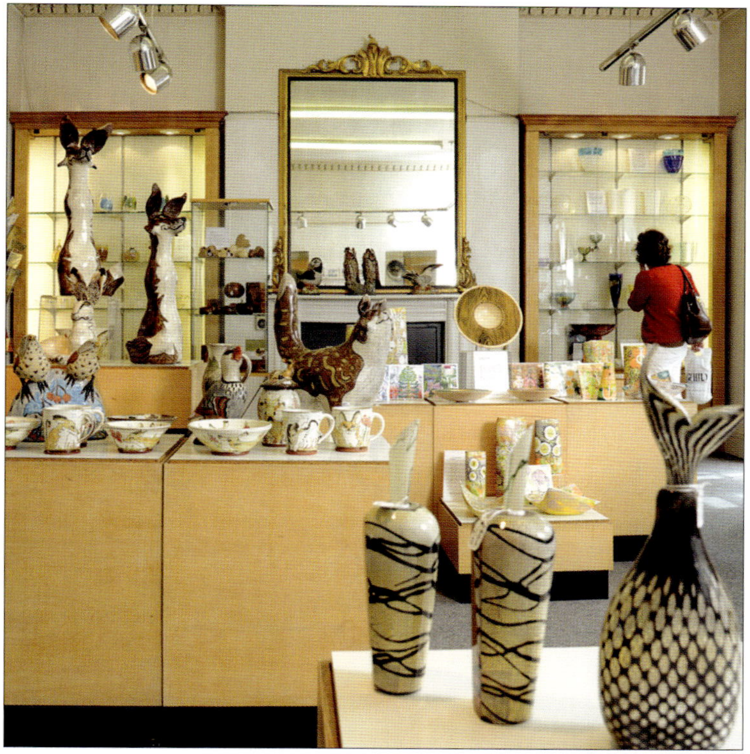

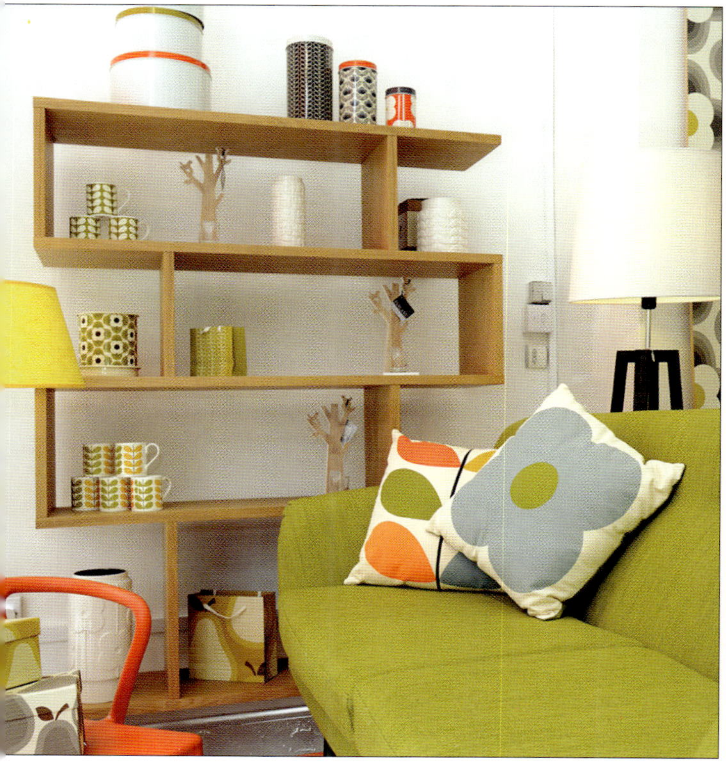

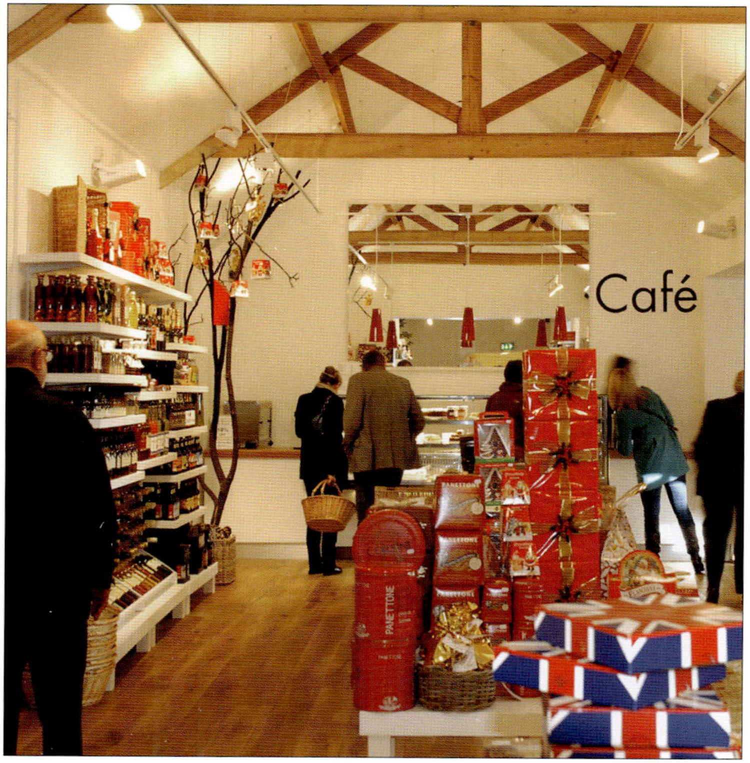
Café

Guild of Applied Art in Park Street, increasing the staff from two to three.

> I was fortunate in that the War gave me the opportunity of changing direction and thinking, I don't want to do this. And then I thought, well, what *do* I want to do? I knew the Guild and so I came into them one day and said, 'you need me, can I join you?' and that's how it all started.

The Guild had originated in 1908 as a collective of artists who promoted and sold their work and offered handicraft classes. Prominent names on the Council included the architect George Oatley. By 1929 the original group had scattered and under its remaining member, stained glass designer Arnold Robinson, the Guild became a small retail shop maintaining its original remit to sell good design and support local makers. In 1948 the Guild's stock was inevitably limited in scope. It was 'a little gift shop… really half a shop, 68A – the other half was a wool shop'. Stradling imposed a strong, creative identity of his own, finding, buying and selling new and innovative work. 'You've got to be in control of the buying', he says, and 'quality is always terribly important ... and you *do* come to recognise quality, with experience it becomes almost intuitive'.

Thus began the transition from survivor of the Arts and Crafts movement to the quirky emporium of

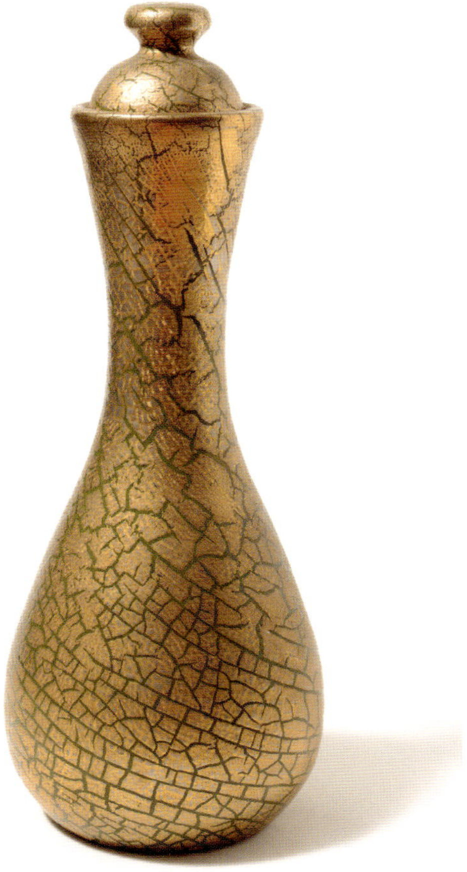

One of the earliest pieces in the Collection, gold crackle Elton vase designed by Sir Edmund Elton of Clevedon, 1907

today. While the 1951 Festival of Britain set out a dynamic modern agenda for architecture and design, economic recovery took time.

> Right through the 1950s it was a terrible time for trade. The only tableware available was plain white but occasssionally one obtained a crate of coloured export rejects which caused great excitement.

Expansion brought with it a furniture department, a restaurant and a food-hall amongst other additions. From the 1960s a gallery space enabled the Guild to present exhibitions of the work of individual artists and designers. The recently completed remodelling of the main stairwell, new food-hall and redesign of the Guild Café with an outside seating area reflects an ongoing process of revision and renewal. The Guild has become a focal point in Bristol and the region for quality design and applied arts.

Ken's business contacts with Scandinavian furniture, glass and ceramics manufacturers provided access to some of the leading work of the post-war period and unusually Ken was able to travel and meet Scandinavian and other European makers, taking a particular interest in Swedish, Danish and Finnish design generally. Alongside the furniture and ceramics by manufacturers such as Arabia, glass became a particular interest and the collection contains many fine pieces by Holmegaard, Orrefors

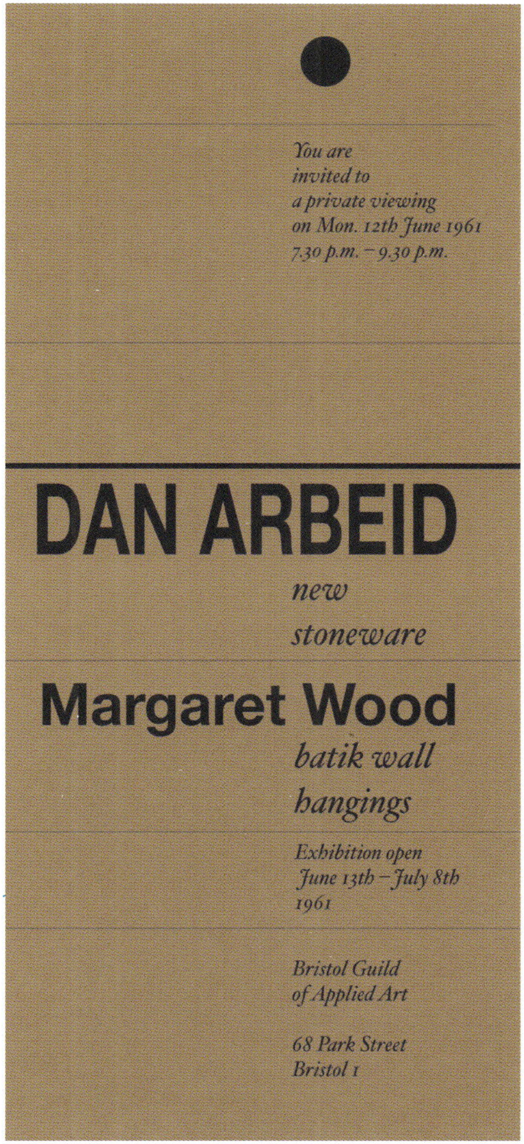

Dan Arbeid's first show outside London: Bristol Guild Gallery, June 1962. Fifty years later the Gallery held a retrospective of his work (over)

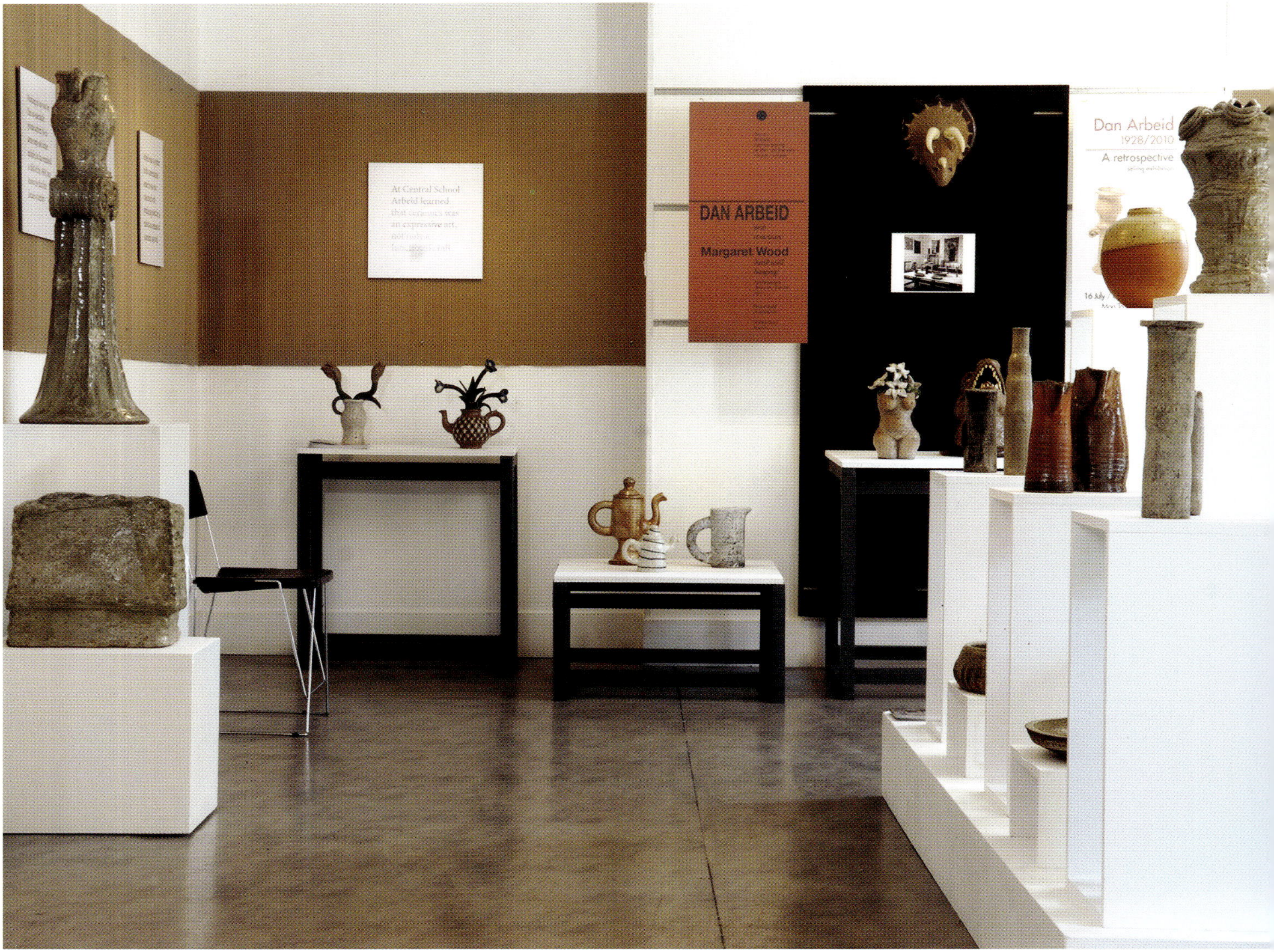

Dan Arbeid Retrospective, Bristol Guild Gallery July 2011

and Whitefriars amongst others. In the 1960s through Betty, Ken was introduced to studio ceramics. Betty had been a student at Corsham College of Art in the 50s and come into contact with the new sculptural ceramicists emerging from the Central School at that time. Their rough, handbuilt sculptural ceramics resonated with the Scandinavian studio glass of the period and, fascinated by their work, Ken made it a key feature of the Collection and the shop. Friendships emerged with the like of Dan Arbeid, Gillian Lowndes, Robin Welch and Ian Auld. Other potters with whom Ken has been friendly for many years and whose work features prominently in his collection include Peter Wright, Dick Freeman, Marianne de Trey and John Leach.

Buying for the Guild brought Ken into contact with the best artists, designers, manufacturers and makers, many of whom became firm friends as well as business partners. Expansion of the Guild and the introduction of a gallery space allowed Ken to be more experimental with the kind of work that he showed. The gallery provided not just a selling opportunity for artists and makers, but was a key means of engaging audiences with new work. The Guild expanded steadily, selling furniture, textiles, jewellery, kitchenware and toys; the gallery displaying crafts and fine arts by mostly West-Country artists. Ken is a passionate advocate for Bristol and the West Country and has been actively involved with many local projects and campaigns, including the ss *Great Britain* Trust and City Docks Ventures. He is a patron of young artists and designers in the region and, fittingly, for many years was chair of the Gane Trust – the fund created by Bristol furniture manufacturer Crofton Gane to provide financial support for young people working in craft, design, the arts and social care in the south west. Ken was deputy chair of the Dartington Cider Press Centre for 10 years.

‘As a young couple living in London we loved to shop at Heals and Dunns. On moving to Bristol in the early 70s we were delighted to discover the Guild. All three brought to the High Street a celebration of good contemporary design, craftsmanship and individual creativity. A joy.’ Jo and Denis Jones

One important part of the Collection comprises 1930s’ Modernist furniture from Crofton Gane, a champion of contemporary design in Bristol. PE Gane Ltd. was an established company making Arts and Crafts-style furniture for middle-class homes. Between the wars Gane used the family business to explore new ideas and materials. He travelled to

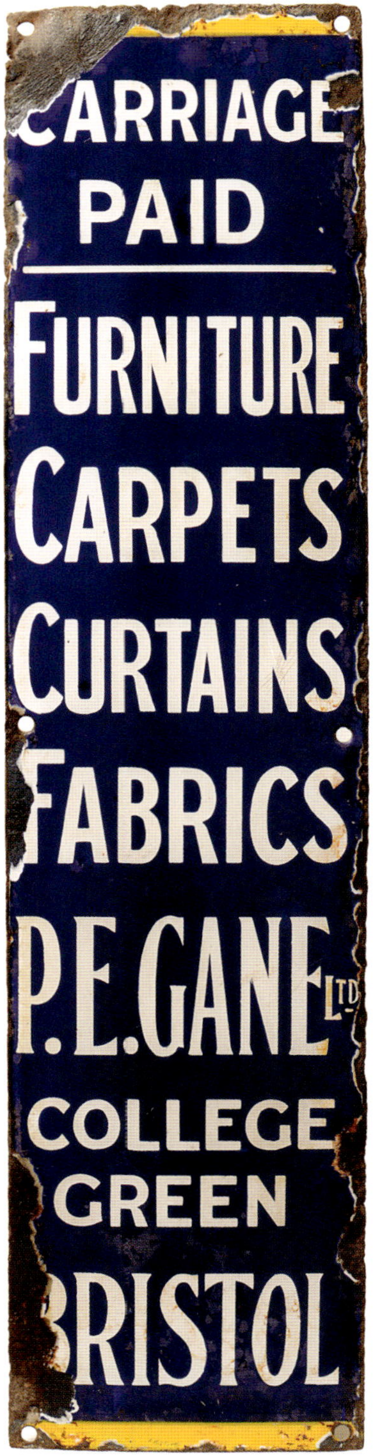

Enamelled sign from PE Gane's shop on College Green, Bristol c.1910

Scandinavia, Holland and Germany and visited the influential 1925 Paris Exhibition. When the leading Bauhaus designer Marcel Breuer arrived in England in 1935, Gane commissioned him to design a pavilion for his company at the 1936 Royal Agricultural Show in Ashton Court, Bristol. Gane also commissioned Breuer to remodel and design furniture for his house in Westbury Park. Much of the content of the house survives and the Ken Stradling Collection has assembled the largest group in any public collection – some 15 pieces including much of the living room furniture. It is the remarkable legacy of an internationally-renowned Bauhaus designer in Bristol.

Furniture, glass, pottery, fine art and crafts, the Ken Stradling Collection is a remarkably diverse entity that reflects the personality and idiosyncracies of one man, an incidental collector who became a patron and a friend to many of the makers represented and who buys things for the pleasure they give him

In 1988, echoing the sentiments of his former headmaster JE Barton, Ken Stradling wrote that:

> the general standard of public taste will never improve until design becomes an integral part of everyone's general education.

Twenty years later, in considering how to make the Collection available to the public, Ken took advice

A home to furnish: a range of carefully chosen pieces including Italian glass, English crafts, a Howard Keith chair (left) and a Charles Eames chair from the USA

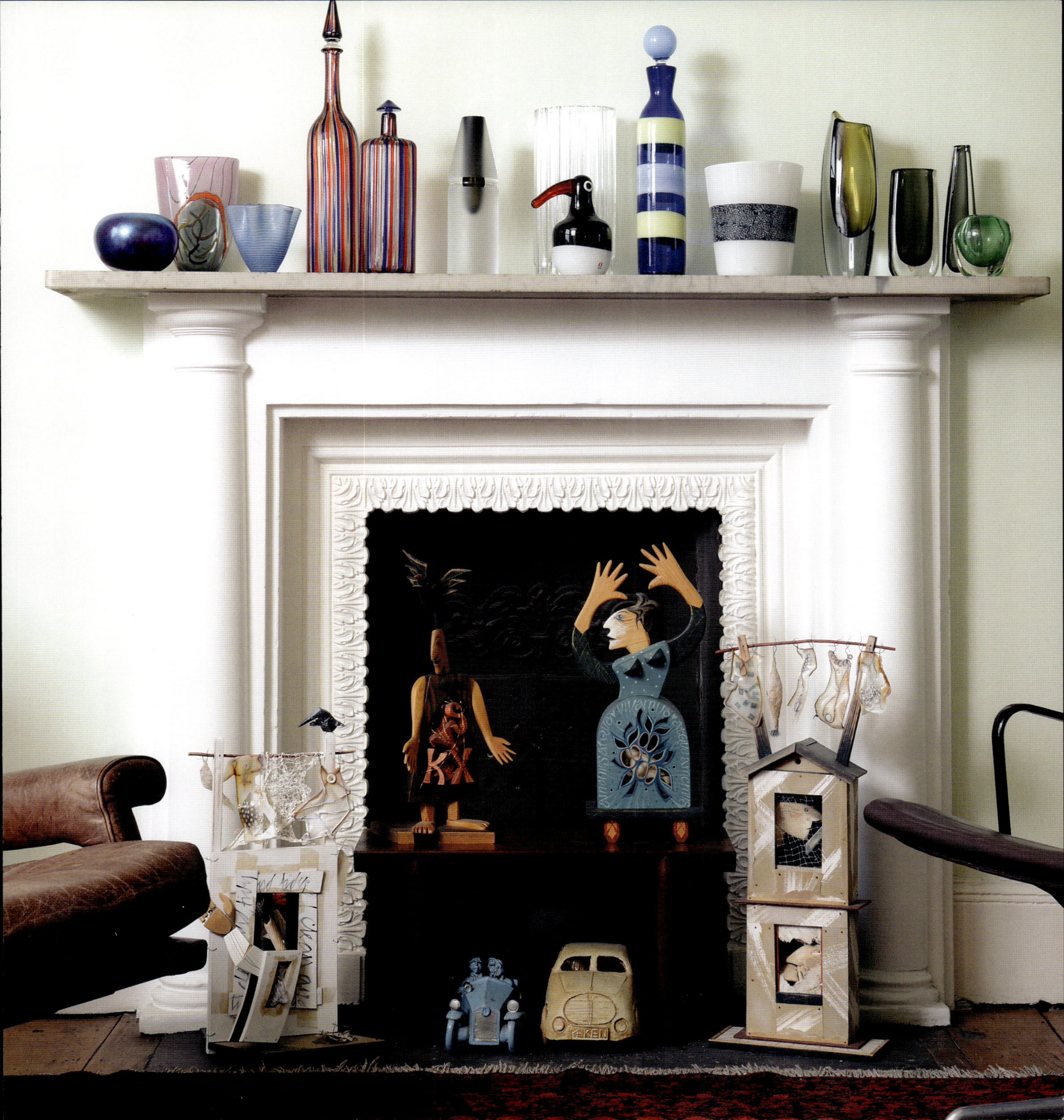
4KEN

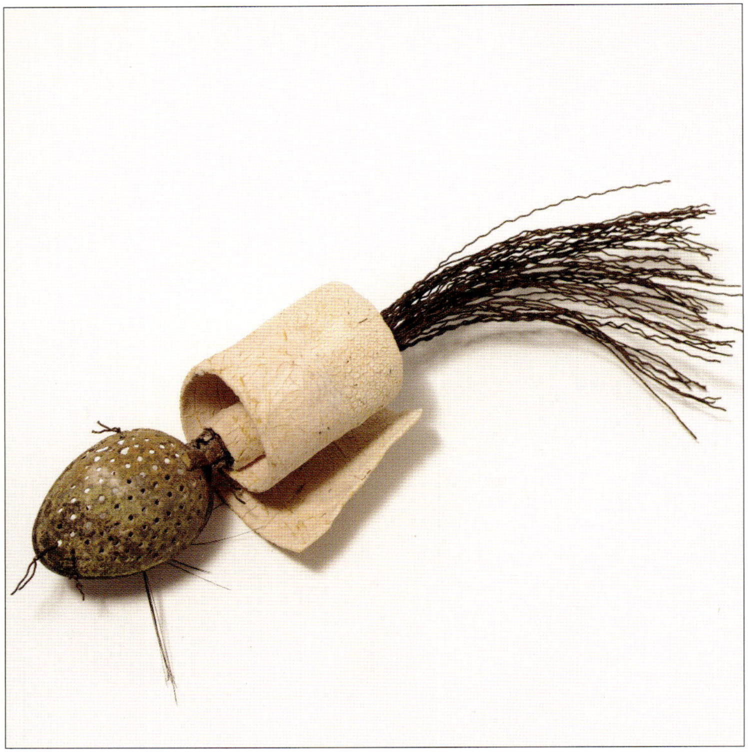
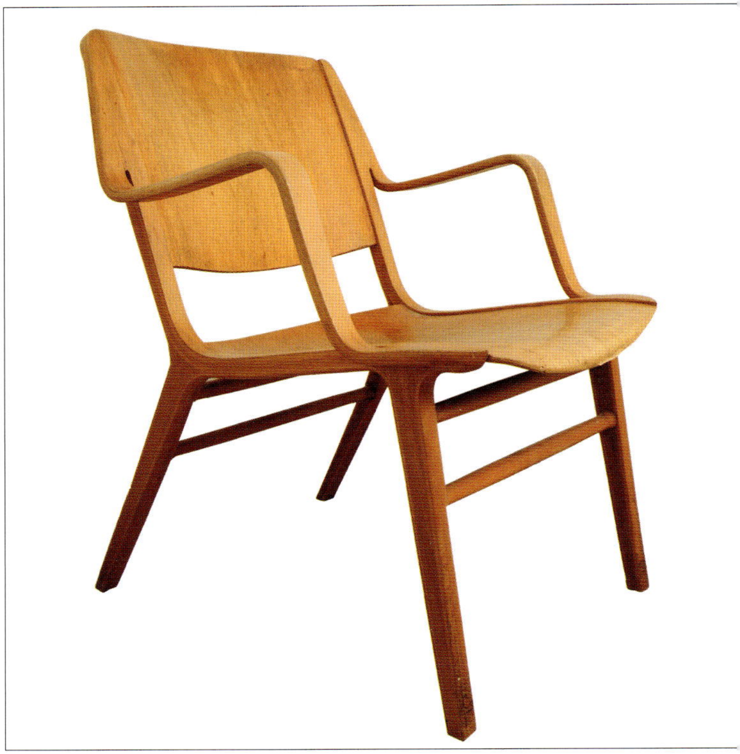
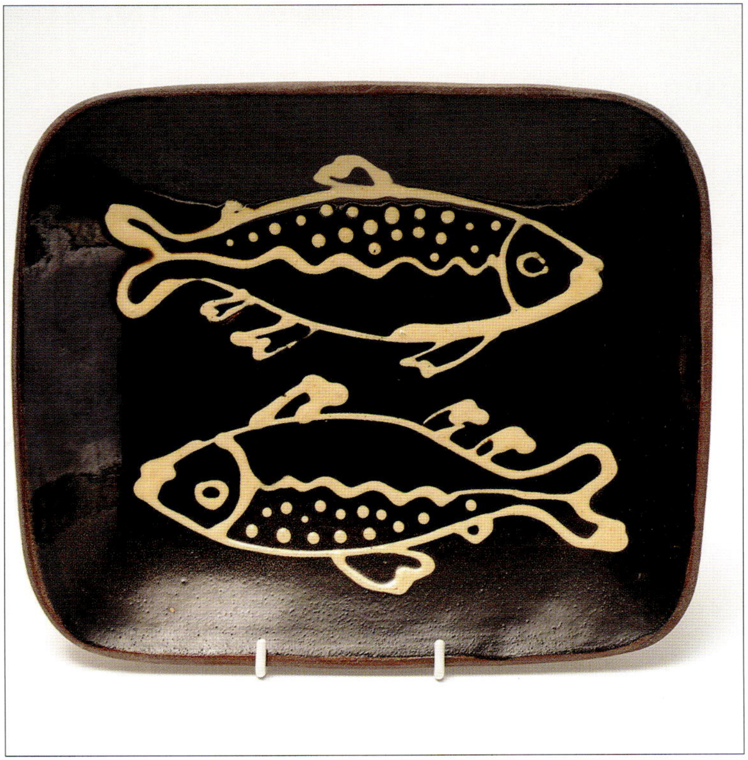
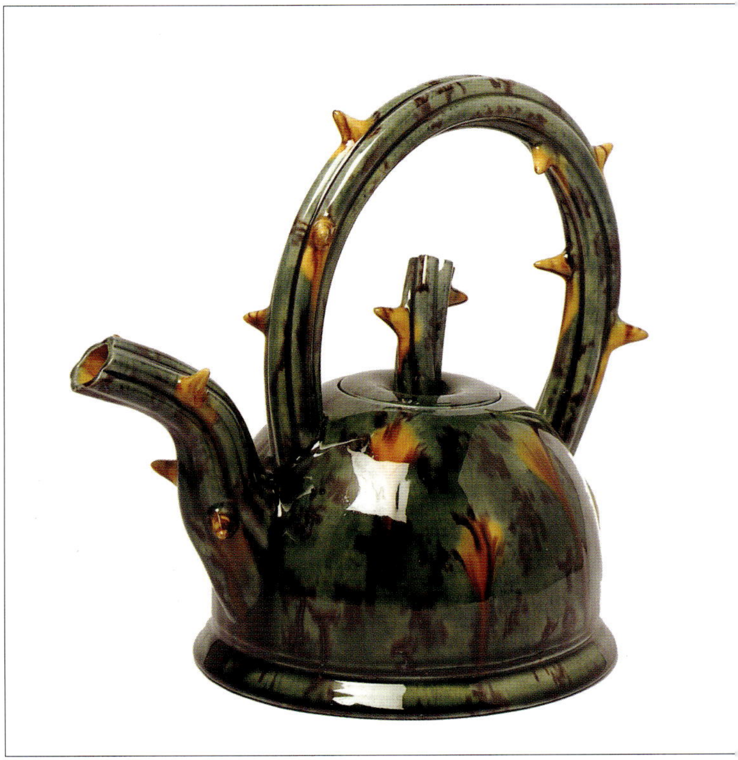

'The Guild was my University,
Ken was my tutor'
Sid Burnard, sculptor

from Christopher Lloyd, June Lancaster, David Whiting and the collector Anthony Shaw.
Rather than offer it to a museum he decided, like Shaw, to create a trust and provide a permanent home for the Collection in an adapted building.

Today, the Ken Stradling Collection Trust exists to care for the Collection and to make it available for everyone to study and enjoy, providing easy access both to the objects and the substantial documentary records and personal archives of the artists and designers. By opening the Collection to everyone – the curious, the student and the practitioner – Ken and the trustees hope to educate, inspire and enlighten present and future generations.

Clockwise from top left: *Small Scroll with Spoon*, slip-dipped fibreglass scroll, fired spoon, and bristles, Gillian Lowndes, 1990s | *Ax* chair, Peter Hvidt and Orla Molgaard-Nielsen, 1954 | earthenware pie-dish, Marianne de Trey, 1949/50 | teapot, Walter Keeler, 2010

'LEARNING TO LOOK'
THE COLLECTION IN PERSPECTIVE

David Whiting

The fine and comprehensive collection of Ken Stradling, particularly rich in ceramics but also interesting for its range of other crafts – glass, wood and furniture – has come into the public eye at a time when the importance of such holdings has been brought to the fore. In the past ten years or so some of the most significant personal collections of studio ceramics have gone public, a fact that has helped refocus our interest in what the acquisitive tastes of individuals can offer to our understanding, as opposed perhaps to the collective curatorial policies of our museums and public collections. Not that collecting studio pottery is such a new phenomenon. It goes back to the second decade of the last century, with early collectors that included Henry Bergen, an American academic based in Britain who became a very competent amateur potter, and the actors Charles Laughton and his wife Elsa Lanchester.

Another important precursor was Dean Eric Milner-White (1884-1963), whose choice group of master-works by pioneering British studio potters was given to the cities of York and Southampton, and is now on show at their respective art galleries. Milner-White purchased his first pot in 1925, and his collection, featuring particularly the major figures of the inter-war years, set a standard. It was a passion that began purely by chance; on impulse he walked into a Bond Street gallery (the Fine Art Society), discovered an exhibition of pots by Reginald Wells and from then on was hooked. Though he bought some table-wares, the collection concentrated on individual pieces, exhibition pots that were essentially works of art – bottles, bowls and dishes by Bernard Leach, the Martin brothers, William Staite Murray, Michael Cardew, Ladi Kwali, Shoji Hamada, Sam Haile and Katharine Pleydell-Bouverie, amongst others. Milner-White's collection reflected a pre-war taste for 'significant form' (to borrow Clive Bell's phrase), the sense that pottery was, or could be, an aspect of pure sculpture.

The late W A Ismay (1910-2001) was another collector-patron who was able to acquire work as it was made. A librarian by profession, and born in Wakefield, he developed his passion for clay in the 1950s, sown in part by his appreciation of traditional potters during his war service in India. Though he

A collector's shelves: a selection arranged by Ken in his sitting room shows the collection's variety, including pieces by James Tower, Erik Höglund, John Maltby and Walter Keeler

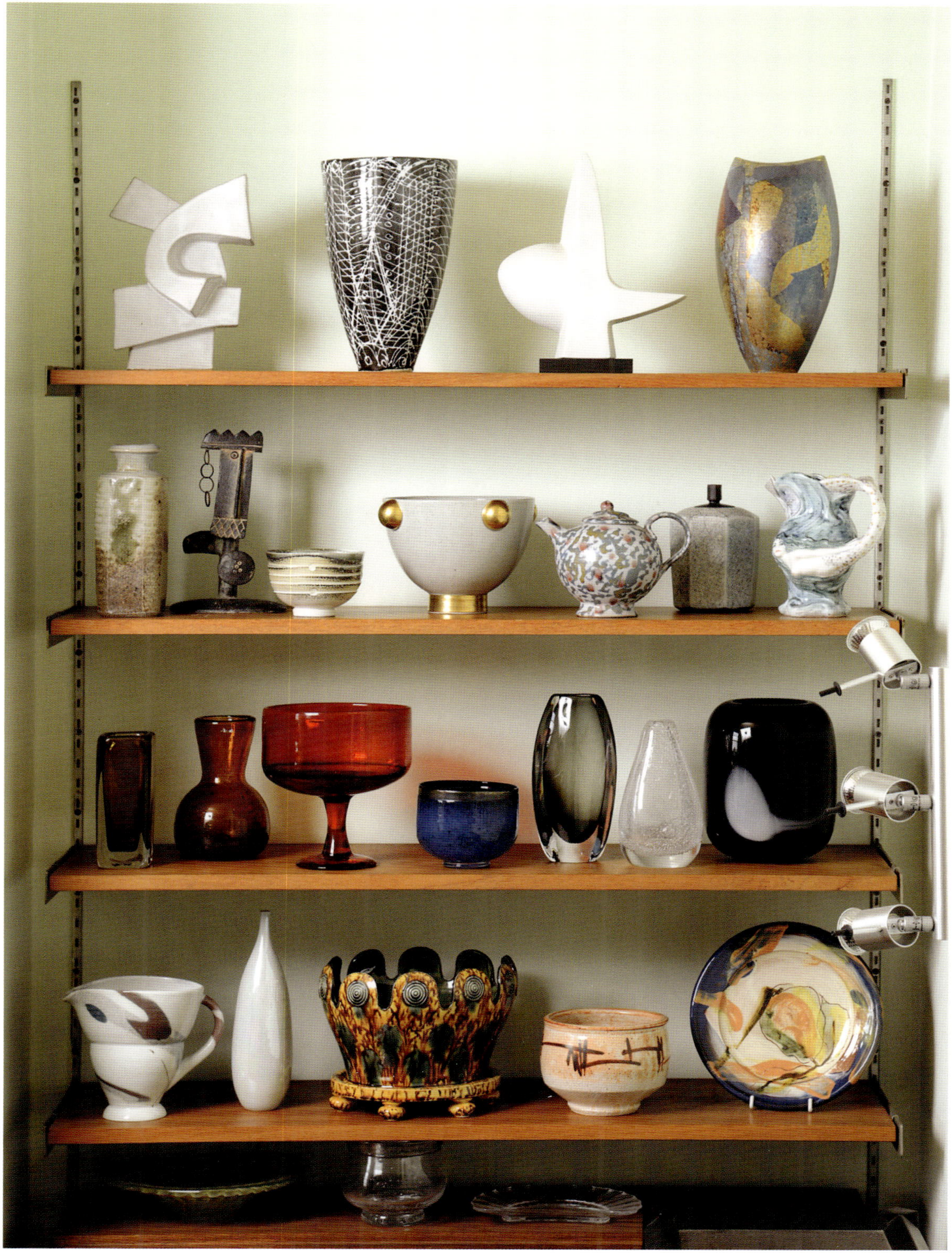

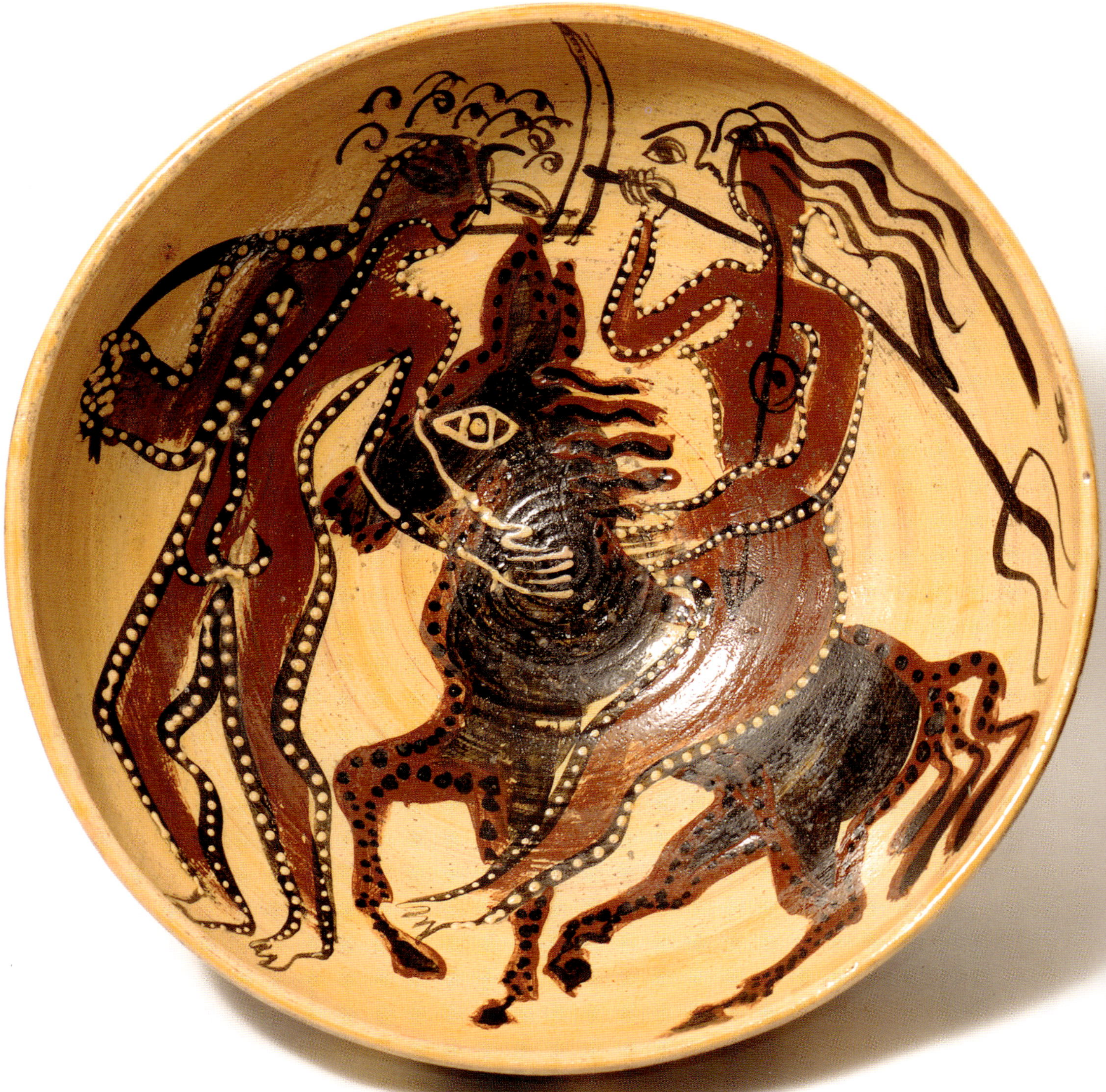

collected during a period in which studio ceramics was expanding into the world of sculpture, Ismay's taste was based, like Milner-White's, in mainly more traditional functionally-based forms, and largely anglo-oriental in inspiration. Yet he also had fine pieces by modernist potters like Lucie Rie and Hans Coper, and made a few forays into more experimental work, perhaps to satisfy his completist tendencies.

Around a solid corpus of pioneer potters – Leach, Cardew, Hamada and so forth – he collected with extraordinary industry large groups (sometimes upwards of sixty pieces) by other favourite artists, and hundreds of token pieces by makers he simply wanted to support, and whose inclusion demonstrated just how the field of British studio ceramics had grown in the period Ismay was active. In addition to a growing apprenticeship system in the workshops, ceramics courses, still scarce after the war, began to proliferate, particularly in the 1960s and 70s. Bill Ismay's passion extended to criticism, particularly for *Ceramic Review*, and he must have travelled thousands of miles by train (he didn't drive) in his pursuit of pots, potters and the latest gallery exhibition. No purchasing queue was complete without him, Ismay haunting galleries and shops like the showroom of the Craft Potters Association, Amalgam in Barnes, and Peter Dingley Gallery in Stratford-upon-Avon. This last shop was also a favourite with another pioneer collector, Rollo Ballantyne (1917-1998), a medical practitioner whose fine holding of mainly functional pots was put into trust in the late 1970s, and after two locations eventually found a permanent home at Nottingham Castle Museum, in the city of his birth.

The more sculptural work emerging from college and studio in the 1950s onwards was soon being acquired by a select group, most notably perhaps Henry Rothschild (1913-2009). Rothschild, a German Jewish émigré, had established his enterprising shop and gallery Primavera in London's Sloane Street in 1946 (followed by a branch in Cambridge – eventually to be his sole premises – in the next decade). Primavera, progressively modern in its choice of stock, was a rare splash of colour in the austere years following the war, and sold crafts of all kinds, from furniture and basketry to glass, textiles and jewellery. Pottery was a particular focus, and the shop would sell functional pieces by, amongst others, Lucie Rie and Hans Coper, Richard Batterham, Geoffrey Whiting, and Harry and May Davis.

He gave early exhibitions to a number of artists associated with the forward-thinking Central School, potters whose work was experimental and more consciously expressive. Ruth Duckworth, Ian Auld, Gillian Lowndes, Ian Godfrey, Dan Arbeid and Gordon Baldwin were all featured in Primavera solo

◀ Slip-decorated bowl,
Sam Haile, 1938

or group shows and many were exhibited in his memorable international exhibitions at Kettles Yard in Cambridge in the 1970s and early 80s. Rothschild's own collection included much of this work, an investigation of clay that related to early and contemporary art and organic forms in nature, and less to the history of ceramics itself. He was still buying adventurously into his early nineties, with his and his wife's rooms in a care home in Oxford stuffed with rare examples by the studio artists who meant most to him.

A young couturier, Anthony Shaw (born 1951), was introduced to the riches of Primavera at an early age by his parents. He had grown up with studio tablewares, much of it bought from Rothschild's London shop, and soon began collecting himself, initially pots but soon moving on to sculptural pieces. He collected Gillian Lowndes, Gordon Baldwin and Ewen Henderson on a scale even greater than Rothschild, but also had a particular interest in younger artists such as Sara Radstone. His patronage extended to organising window displays of new ceramics in his West Kensington shop. Both Shaw and Rothschild followed very particular instincts, aware that clay could do interesting things outside 'conventional' pottery, and just as Ismay championed more traditional forms, these collectors were fascinated by its possibilities beyond containment.

While Bill Ismay's collection was more democratic and inclusive (one might even argue that he was an inveterate ceramic hoarder, seemingly unwilling to de-accession even the weakest of his purchasing decisions), Shaw's and Rothschild's became increasingly focussed. Highly individual though these holdings certainly are, with different motivations guiding each collector, all three have now joined Milner-White's at York Art Gallery (with a larger share of Rothschild's having already gone to the Shipley Art Gallery in Gateshead). So now we can judge their riches for ourselves, and we may also get a clearer insight into the fertile minds that have shaped them. But of course their original context has been lost, the sense of 'place' that we get when we see these objects in their original, highly individual localities. They are absorbed into a certain neutrality, that of the curatorial space, separated to some extent from the idiosyncrasies of the collector's eye and hand. The Stradling Collection may now too be preserved for the future, but it will retain its independence, remaining in the place that helped to form it, so that its unique un-rarefied backcloth of a busy retail space will remain integral.

Ken Stradling touched on the visual rewards of such acquisition when he said 'learning to look can be as creative as making', a philosophy that has guided the whole principle of his working life. Stradling (born 1922) arrived as an employee of the Bristol Guild,

Another grouping in Ken's home on a Gordon Russell sideboard, including *Model 78* chairs by Niels Moller, 1962, drawings by Sam Smith and painting by Anna Teasdale

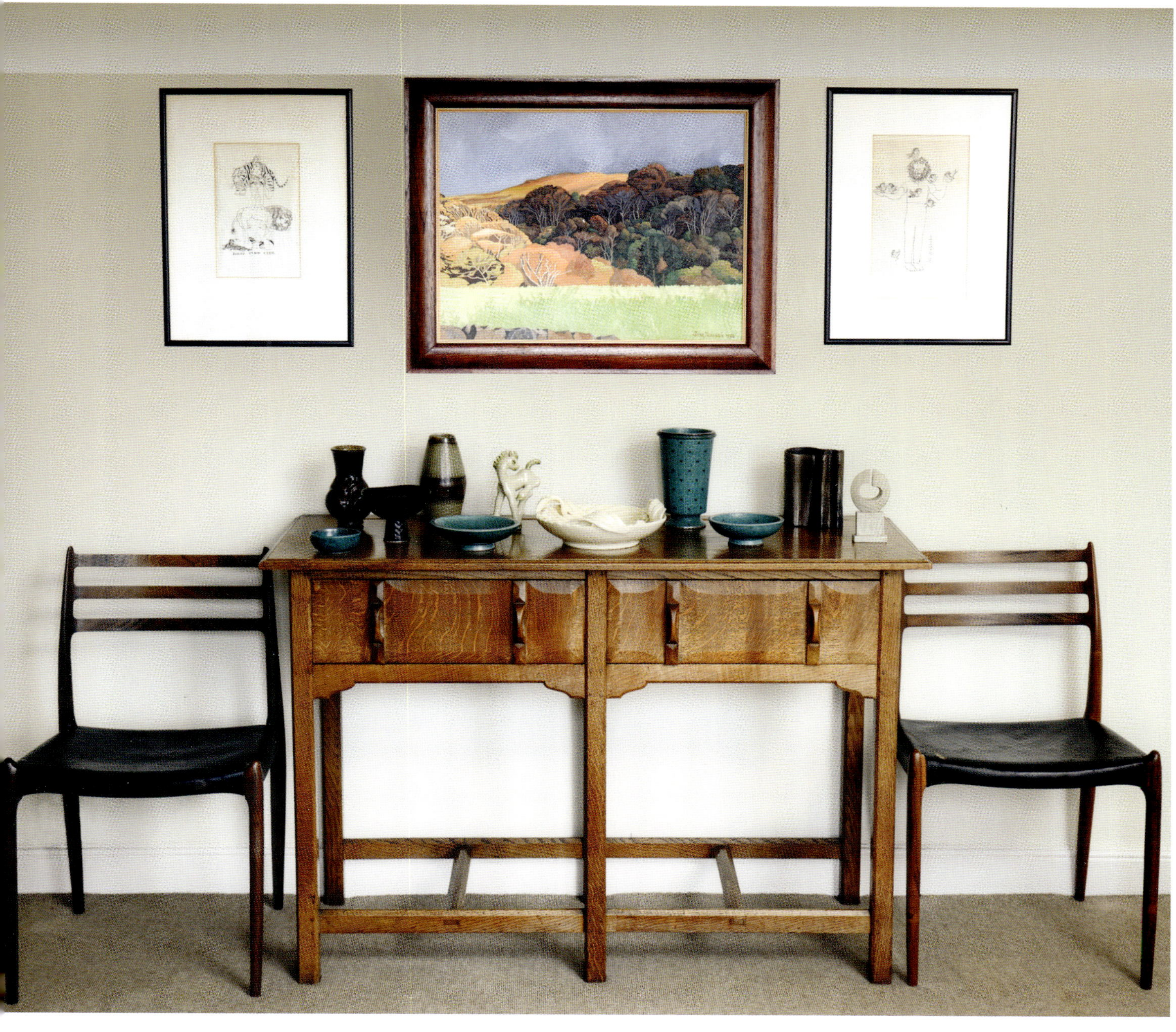

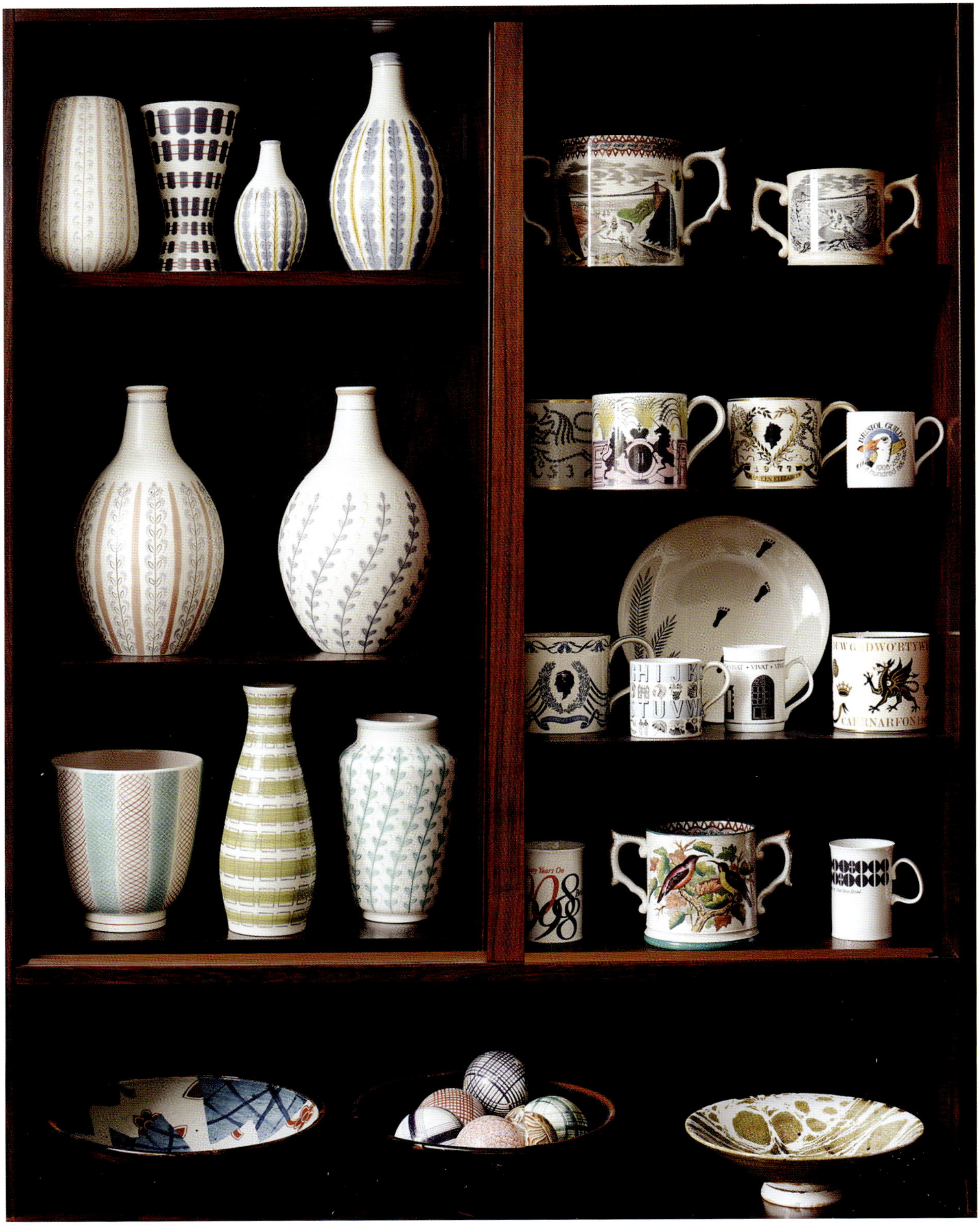
BRISTOL GUILD

then a relatively small retail enterprise, in 1948, just two years after Rothschild opened Primavera. Like Rothschild he developed his collecting eye and expertise through his profession. They were both ex-servicemen who had learnt through direct, one might say empirical research, in buying for their shops. While Rothschild had procured the hand-list of crafts men and women from the Rural Industries Bureau, and toured the country in search of products before he set up, Ken Stradling, whose initial interest was mainly in furniture, was very keen to broaden the choice of goods at the Guild, and began his own investigations, much of it also by travel.

In the austere post-war years the Guild was dealing primarily in utility products and export rejects, a meagre ration for those needing fresh visual stimulus. Stradling quickly developed a considerable knowledge of craft and design, not least because of his wife Betty, a painter who had trained at nearby Corsham School of Art who brought him into direct contact with numerous painters and potters. He had began buying odd pieces of pottery as a young man, for example items made at Edmund Elton's pioneering Clevedon workshop, just down the road. But it was really glass that nurtured his initial acquisitive instincts, particularly the more functional forms. Though his collection as it developed had a distinct and evolving shape, it grew more by stealth than strategy, with purchases made steadily but not always consistently, with regrets later that he didn't necessarily buy for himself artists he stocked and exhibited at the Guild. Many of these gaps have since been filled by judicious purchasing from auction houses, a means by which he has also made the collection more generally representative of the studio ceramics story, but also the taste he was exercising at his shop.

Like Rothschild, Stradling's knowledge and buying and collecting taste loosely reflected the kind of objects being copiously illustrated in the *Studio Year Book of Decorative Art*, one of the few publications available in the 1950s and 60s that celebrated current design and craft, and was distinctly international in scope. Rothschild's and Stradling's preferences shared some of the same Continental trends, with a particular emphasis on what Scandinavia had to offer, a culture which put object design into a strong architectural context. They were certainly regional pioneers, helping to introduce a visually undernourished country to some of the best forms being produced in mainland Europe. In Rothschild's house in Cambridge there were pots and other objects covering surfaces and filling extensive cupboard space, seen in the context of good modern furniture and paintings, not so dissimilar to Stradling's Bristol home. And if Bill Ismay's collection was so vast that it occupied every inch of his small terraced Wakefield house (so

Shelves in Ken's study hold Poole 'Contemporary' vases from the 1950s designed by A B Rhead and Guy Sydenham and Wedgwood mugs with designs by Eric Ravilious

becoming little more than storage space), Anthony Shaw's equally modest London home, put into trust and opened to the public before the collection went to York, showed ceramics in their domestic world with fabrics, paintings, books and drawings as a backdrop. People could appreciate the natural dialogue between one object and another, part of a visual (and tactile) whole.

Stradling's ceramics collection grew out of a corpus of early hand-built and thrown pieces by the likes of Gillian Lowndes, Dan Arbeid and Robin Welch, showing, like Rothschild, how attracted he was to the aesthetic that had grown up amongst artists and teachers around the Central School and Institute of Education in London. In parallel there was the comparable work of distinguished local potters like Peter Wright (who also taught at Corsham) and Richard Freeman, whose sculptural forms and functional wares were also championed by Stradling. He made early contact with most of these figures, with Lowndes, Welch, Arbeid, Wright and Freeman all being given major early exhibitions at the Bristol Guild, an association that often lasted many years. He had a preference for their free and direct approach to the clay, so different to the more lyrical forms of the Leach school, with which pottery was more readily associated. There was an emphasis on the clay itself, often devoid of a covering glaze, the surfaces qualities perhaps accentuated instead by a slip or oxide. There was also an often totemic, other-worldly aspect to such work, clearly seen in some of the objects Gillian Lowndes showed at the Guild in 1963, her first solo exhibition, and like Dan Arbeid's two years earlier (following his first showing at Primavera), one of the key events at that time that indicated ceramics was taking a new and exciting direction.

His attraction to the materiality of an object extended to his blown glass purchases. Makers like Sam Herman and Erik Högland explored similarly unrefined textures, the forms bold and elemental. And along with elegant pieces of Venini from Venice, Holmegaard from Denmark, Orrefors and Kosta Boda from Sweden (the former sold at the Guild since since the early years of the last century) and London's Whitefriars, such work has sat easily on the robust simple furniture designs in Ken's varied collection of, most notably, Gordon Russell, Alan Peters, Alvar Aalto, Ernest Race and Marcel Breuer. Whitefriars and Herman glass were prominently featured too at Primavera, largely no doubt because of the innate modernity of the forms, whether studio or factory made. Both Stradling and Rothschild were appreciative of the ethos of the 1951 Festival of Britain, but were not so interested in some of its more flamboyant visual excesses. In terms of furniture, Scandinavia and 'Danish Modern' appealed because of the clean forms and the solid and honest

Wooden box by Howard Raybould, 1999.
10" x 10" x 9" (25 x 25 x 23cm)

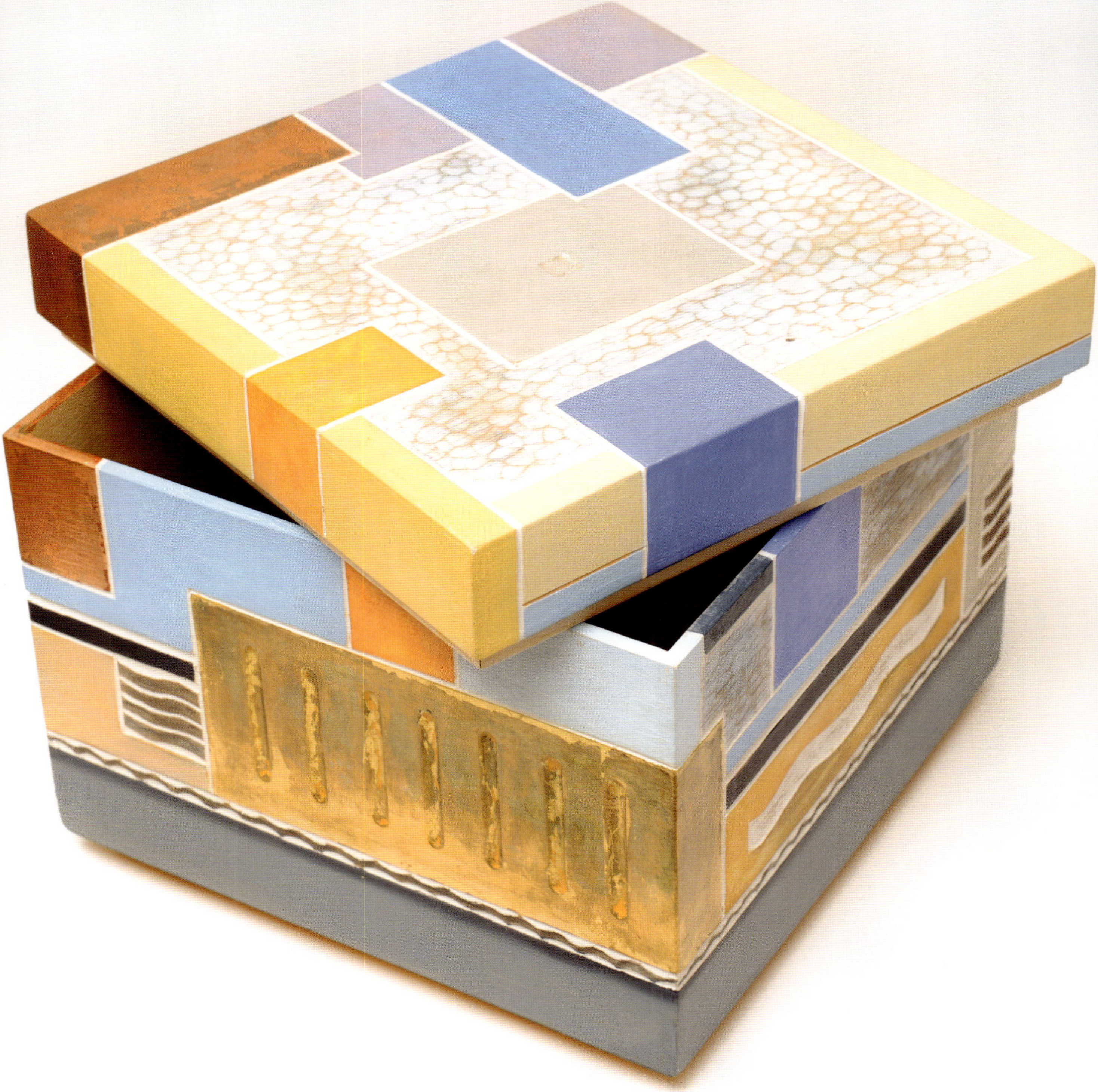

Enamelled steel bowls, Herbert Krenchel, Krenit, Denmark, 1953 | Tea caddy, Peter Cudden, 1960s | *Mon Amie* jug, Marianne Westman, Rorstrand, Sweden, 1966/7

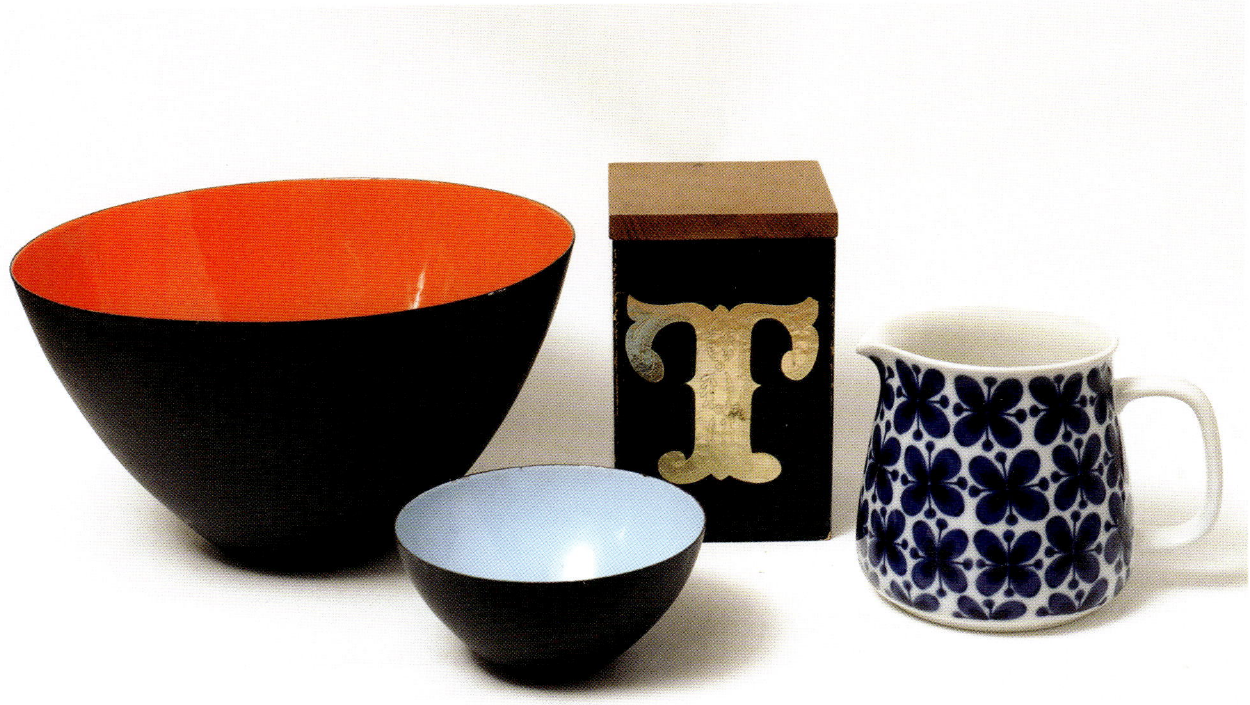

use of the wood and other materials. In fact a Ruskinian 'truth to materials' has been important to both men, but neither Rothschild nor Stradling have had 'any quarrel with industry' (as the former put it, in conversation with the author), both selling and collecting items made in a variety of factories along with handcraft, a result of their egalitarian non-doctrinaire stance. The object should stand or fall on its own merits, regardless of where it was made.

Functional pottery was a retail mainstay of the Bristol Guild. Stradling was one of the first to sell Marianne de Trey's well-designed tableware, first taking her work just after she had established her Devon pottery in 1948, and giving her several solo shows. He built up a good range of her individual pieces in his collection, and has since purchased fine pots by her late husband Sam Haile, as well as William Newland (like Haile, exemplary in slipware) and

James Tower, both closely associated with the Central and the Institute of Education. In recent years he has strengthened his holding of throwers, with pieces by, for example, Michael Cardew, Ray Finch, Richard Batterham, Geoffrey Whiting, Walter Keeler and David Miller. There is imaginative figuration by the much neglected William Gordon, and John Maltby. From a younger generation there is Matthew Blakely and Kevin de Choisy. But such hand-made work stands seamlessly and democratically with factory wares, with styles and idioms as diverse as Arabia from Finland, and, closer to home, Pountney's Bristol Pottery and Poole. The Bristol Guild was a major agent for Poole, with Stradling a particular admirer of the designs of AB Rhead. He could see the strong design relationship of Poole at this time with Stig Lindberg's equally spirited work with Gustavsberg in Sweden. Ken's taste for often colourful and decorative ceramics was extended into his passion for more decorative studio glass (Annette Meech for example) and wooden figuration, with inventive and playful artists like Sam Smith, Peter Markey and Eleanor Glover. Smith's narrative whimsy delighted Rothschild too, in some ways a contemporary realisation of the traditional folk pieces and toys he also sold at his shop. Wooden Scandinavian toys have been a delightful find in the Bristol Guild over the years. Howard Raybould's solid, often more geometric pieces, vividly painted, have extended Ken Stradling's personal enjoyment of the material's natural warmth, and was another artist he showed for a long period.

Once an object is made it goes out into the world and has to fight for itself. In a collection such as Ken Stradling's, every form takes on a new visual meaning, affected by its fresh context, by what surrounds it. Collections are evolving ever-transforming organisms because of this, richly hybrid in their nature. Ken Stradling's unique holding of modern craft and design tells a very particular story, in many ways an autobiography of both his professional and private passions, and a real insight into a life busily promoting as well as acquiring such work. And although ceramics are given priority, it is their relationship to other objects in a variety of media that makes this rich accumulation so particularly personal and intimate. It moves away from the purism and perhaps limitations of acquiring just one material. And in setting up a trust which will safeguard this collection for all to enjoy, Bristol will be provided with a wonderful resource at a time when our society needs to place much more emphasis on visual literacy from an early age. And visual literacy is what Ken Stradling, both as retailer and collector, has spent a lifetime helping to spread.

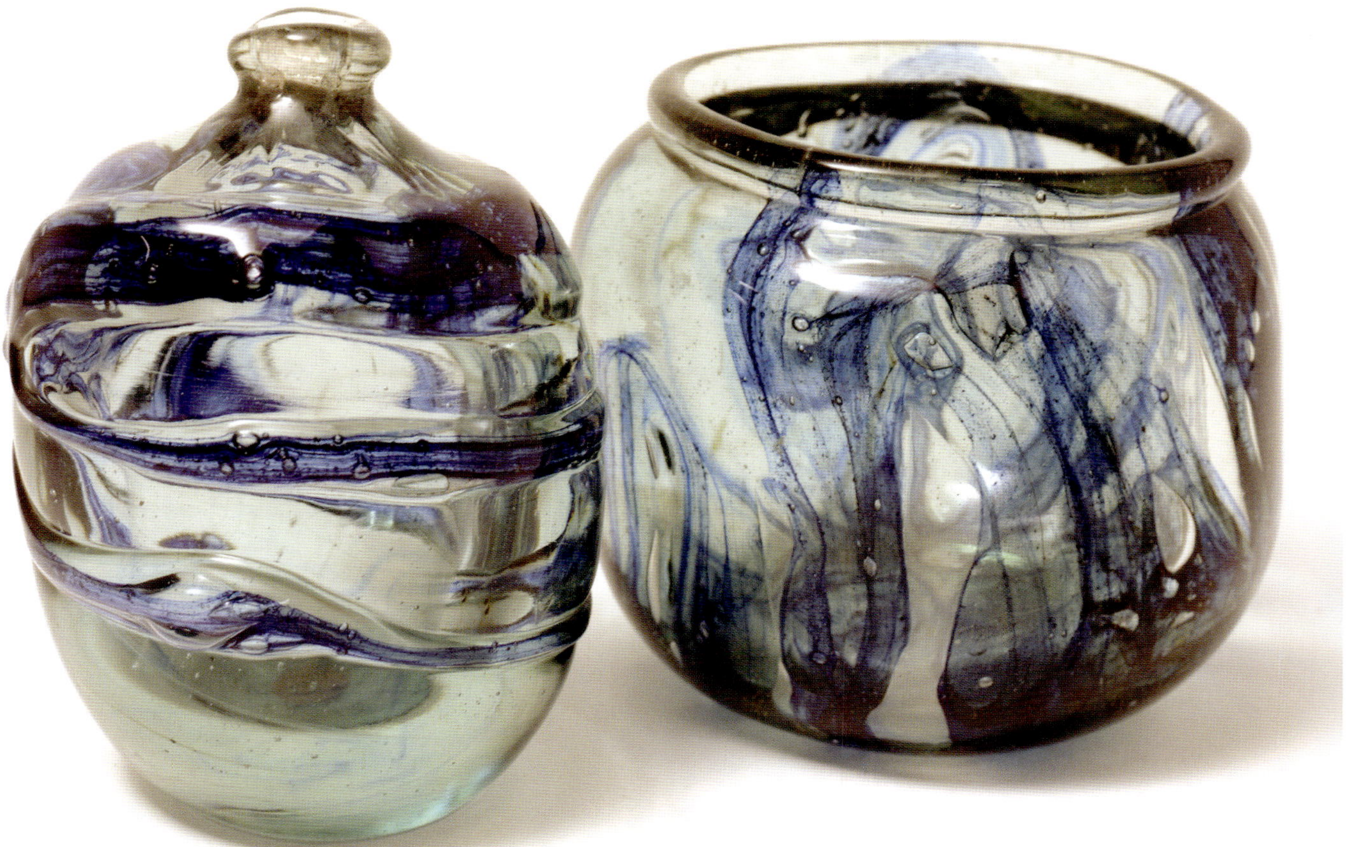

Free-blown glass by Sam Herman, c.1967. Part of ‘a deliberate attempt to rediscover an innocent and unsophisticated glass language’

BUYING, SELLING AND COLLECTING POST-WAR GLASS

Graham McLaren

> You get very sensitive to what's going on.[1]

Of all the design areas represented in the Stradling Collection, glass is arguably closest to Ken's heart. As such the collection represents a valuable insight into personal collecting habits and tastes, but it is the way that these pieces offer a window into the world of post war retail buying and selling that particularly interests me.

When Stradling arrived at the Bristol Guild as buyer in 1948, the selling of high quality glass products was already very much at the heart of the firm's trade. The Guild was, for example already an official outlet for the Swedish glass firm of Orrefors. For that reason his approach to buying glass initially continued existing relationships as well as forging new ones. Ken has been anxious to reflect this in the collection. An example is the recently acquired set designed by Simon Gate for Orrefors in the early 1920s. Marketed in the United Kingdom by a number of firms including Heal's of London as well as The Bristol Guild, the design was sufficiently popular to survive in production into the mid 1960s.

The representation of pre-war glass in the collection is quite limited though. Stradling is anxious to emphasise that he never collected merely to 'fill in the gaps' and that instead personal taste and a fascination with design has played a much larger role in its formation. Pre-war pieces like the example of Nailsea glass he keeps at home are instead important as links to a family fascination with the decorative arts. This undoubtedly played a significant formative role; frequent visits to shops and auctions with his mother were a regular part of his school days, as was the daily journey to the Bristol Grammar School, taking him past the Guild's showrooms.

Ken arrived at the Guild understanding therefore that to find the best new design to sell, one had to travel and to search. The Britain of 1948 was an austere place where the availability of goods was limited by a perilous economic situation and the continuing government imposed Utility scheme.

The Stradling Collection contains a good representative collection of Whitefriars glass from the late 1940s and 1950s,[2] as it was still available on the

1 Interview with Ken Stradling, 20/08/12.

2 These examples include the now sought after ribbon-trailed designs by William Wilson.

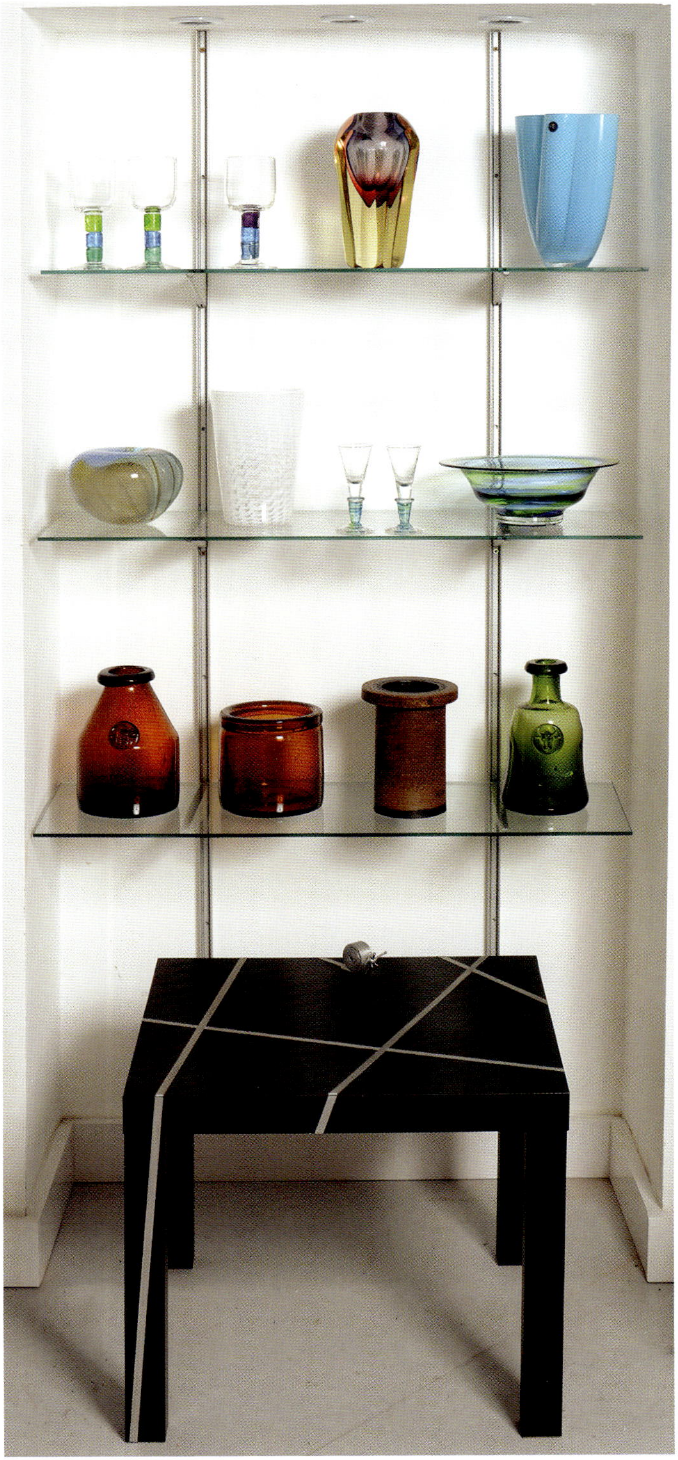

A changing display of glass in the Design Study Centre

domestic market. It also represented a tangible link between post-war British Modern and the original ambitions of the Bristol Guild when it was set up in 1908, namely making and selling goods reflecting the philosophy of the Arts and Crafts Movement. The pieces that we see here reflect a determination to maintain the direction evoked in the mid 1930s by Whitefriars' designer James Hogan:

> Decoration should never be made the sole reason for anything, but there is no reason why – if it adds to the beauty of the design, and is used with restraint – it should not emphasize still more the qualities of the material to which it is applied: those three pre-eminent qualities in the miracle of glass:
>
> Its purity of colour;
> its brilliance; and
> its ductility when heated.[3]

One of the greatest casualties of these austerity years was colour. An approach by historians of design to this period is to contrast the colourlessness of products of the Utility Scheme period,[4] with the explosion of colour in production after it, fuelled by

---

3 De La Valette, John, (Ed) *The Conquest of Ugliness: A Collection of Contemporary Views on the Place of Art in Industry*. Methuen and Co., 1935, pp.151-2.

4 The chemical oxides needed to produce colour in glass were strictly rationed during this period.

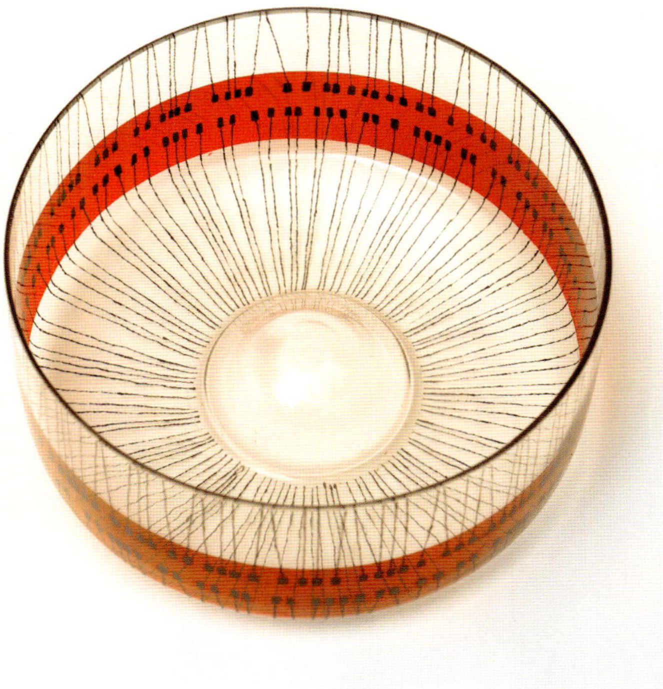

Glass bowl by Zdena Strobachová bought by Ken and Betty Stradling in Czechoslovakia in 1961

public demand for a New Look in household goods as well as fashion. The range of glass in the Stradling Collection certainly seems to reflect this tendency as it is dominated by bright, colourful objects that have often been decorated whilst the glass has been in its hot, plastic state. Ken admits his interest in colour in glass although he is keen to emphasise that this doesn't extend to painted glass, which doesn't appeal to him.[5] Most of the glass therefore looks more to the soda glass making tradition of Venice rather than the lead-glass making and cutting traditions associated with Britain. Cut and engraved glass on display comes instead from the Scandinavian industry and firms such as Orrefors and Stromberg. These are some of the earlier items in the collection, and exemplify the sort of high quality Scandinavian products sold through the Guild's showrooms. Markedly absent are examples of the highly-cut British lead crystal and the ubiquitous press-moulded facsimiles of it that continued to be available in Britain throughout the post-war period.

Ken's thirst for colour can be seen in a highly coloured bowl, a souvenir from an early (c.1961) visit to Czechoslovakia with his wife Betty. The couple were rare western visitors to the country during this period, and Czech glass appears infrequently in the collection as it was not sold at the Guild. However, regular visits to Scandinavia from 1958 were more influential and link to Ken's interests in Scandinavian design more generally. Pieces from Sweden represent the work of Orrefors, Kosta and Skruf; from Norway Hadeland; from Denmark Holmegaard;[6] and from Finland Nuutajärvi and Iittala. Particular favourites for Stradling include the large, free-blown Bamboo Vase by Finnish designer Oiva Toikka for Nuutajärvi. This was purchased by Ken through

5 Interview with Ken Stradling, 20/08/12

6 'The very first trip I did was a trip to Copenhagen to see the Holmegaard glass works. I can remember very clearly that you went into this vast single storey shed as far as the eye could see and there were about twenty glassmaking stations there, with five or six people working in each…' 20/08/12.

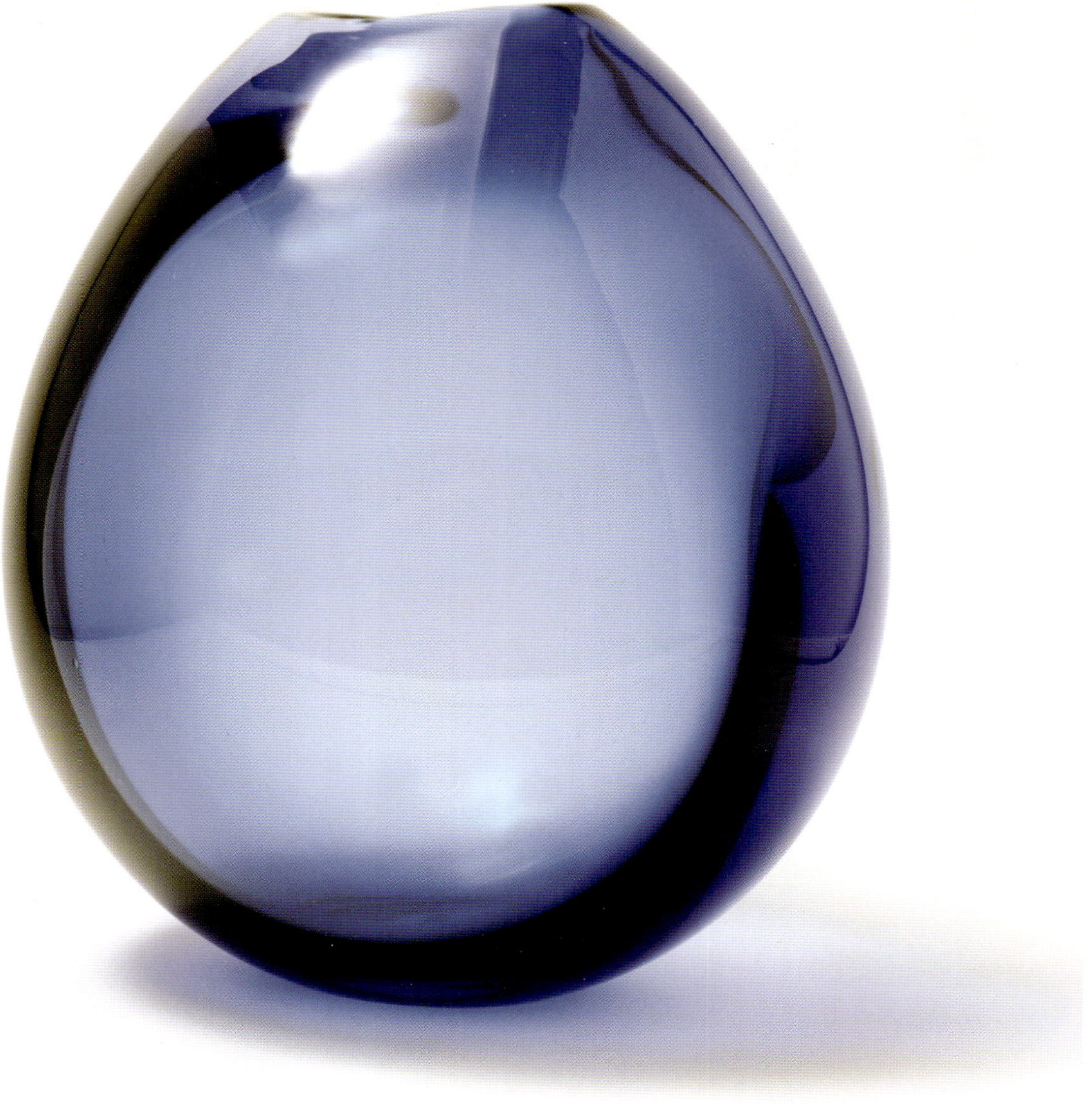

Soap Bubble, Per Lutken, Holmegaard, Sweden, 1961

Swedish glass by Erik Höglund from the 1960s with a stoneware jar by Dan Arbeid, 1973

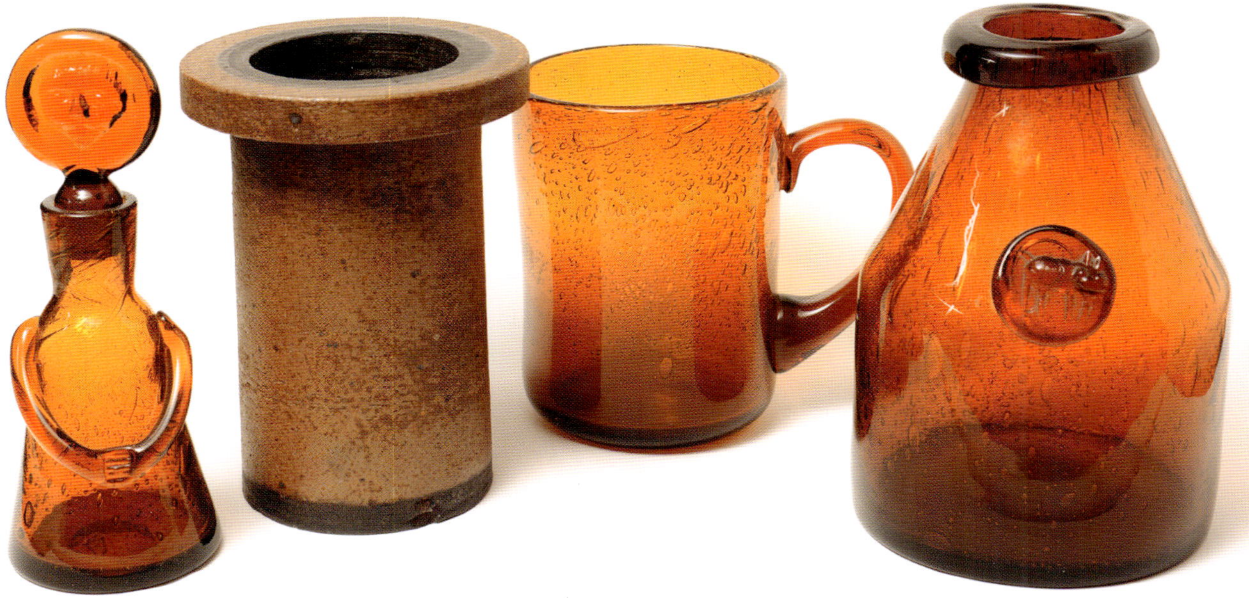

Danasco, who were the '...big importers of everything Scandinavian.'[7] Also notable is an example of Skruf glass by Bengt Edenfalk, appreciated for its free trailed decoration, nestling alongside a couple of Timo Sarpaneva's 'Festivo' candlesticks for Iittala on his sideboard as well as a large example of Per Lütken's 'soap bubble' vase range – 'Very simple, but a lovely piece'.

Stradling's acquiral of objects for his collection is intimately interwoven with his professional life as a buyer. Ken is anxious to emphasise that 'I only ever bought things that I liked' and 'I never bought to a market'.[8] He was also concerned to be ahead of public taste, 'You have to buy what people don't even know that they want...that's terribly important'.[9] An example of this is the substantial presence of work by Eric Höglund. These heavy brown pieces contrast markedly with the prevalent Scandinavian Modern, representing '...a deliberate attempt to rediscover an innocent and unsophisticated glass language'.[10]

7 Ibid, 20/08/12.

8 Ibid.

9 Ibid.

10 Hawkins Opie, J., *Scandinavia: Ceramics and Glass in the Twentieth Century*. Victoria and Albert Museum, 1989, p.103.

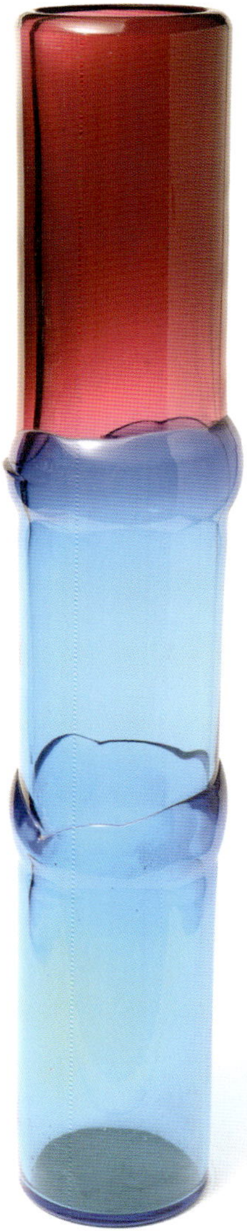

Bamboo vase, Oiva Troikka for Nuutajärvi Nötsö, 1960s/70s

> The point was that just as when Betty introduced me to [Dan] Arbeid etcetera, they were breaking away from the Leach tradition, so Eric Höglund was breaking away from the very refined, elegant Scandinavian glass and doing big, chunky pieces of glass. So that was a parallel and I found that very interesting, and we used to sell a lot of his glass.[11]

Buying what would sell was, of course, central to Stradling's task at the Guild. There were always frustrations with the conservatism of the local market,[12] and there was also pressure (particularly from the design and interiors magazines that periodically reviewed the Guild's goods) to push to the foreground what was 'new', but this could never be at the expense of quality.

Ken acknowledges the freedom he was given, having complete control of buying and never having to work to a budget. This may explain why there was 'always room for a bit of fun'[13] in his purchasing, exemplified within the collection by examples of Italian glass. Well represented here is the firm of Venini. A recently acquired stoppered glass bottle by Fulvio Bianconi takes pride of place on Ken's living room mantelpiece. Next to it stand a brace of 'cane'

11 Interview 20/08/12.

12 Stradling: 'It didn't affect the buying, but it irritated us a lot'. Pre-war Bristol had a reputation as the 'commercial travellers graveyard'. Interview 20/08/12.

13 Ibid.

decanters (*see back cover*), a mainstay of the firm's production from the late 1950s. The decanters had been stocked by the Guild, and Ken had admired but not bought them at the time. By contrast Bianconi's pieces had been too expensive for the Guild to sell, this piece acquired because 'I simply love it'.[14] Bianconi's work is represented again in the large handkerchief vase (designed with Paolo Venini).[15]

Returning to glass production in the United Kingdom, an area of strength for the collection are objects representing a flurry of activity around hot glass-making from the late 1960s onwards. Sam Herman's work, first in education at the Royal College of Art and then at The Glasshouse, the London workshop that he founded in 1969, developed an approach that had its genesis in late 1950s America. It epitomizes a belief that 'a blistered, mottled, collapsed, unidentifiable hand-blown glass object may be more valuable than a crystal swan.'[16] Herman's students and co-workers represented in the collection include pieces by Pauline Solven and a free-blown bowl form by Annette Meech.

Examples like these remind us that the glass in the Stradling Collection is important not only because of

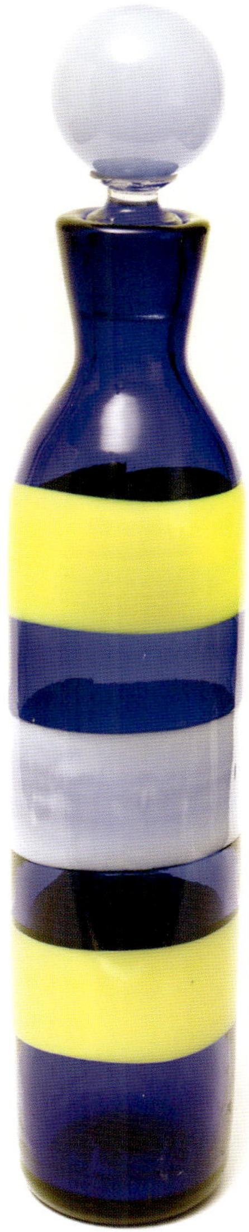

Decanter, Fulvio Bianconi, Venini, Italy, 1950s

---

14 Ibid.

15 The Stradling Collection also has a good selection of the subsequent industrial derivatives of this form produced by industrial firms like Chance Brothers.

16 Harvey Littleton quoted in McLaren, G., *Studio Glass 1960-2000*. Shire, 2002, p.12.

the objects themselves, but also because of the career-long interest that Ken took in individual designers and artists in glass. These objects represent a network of acquaintances and friendships that evoke the inter-relationships that underpinned the post-war glass 'scene'. Ronald Stennett-Willson for instance, was well known to Stradling as an employee of Wuidart, another firm importing Scandinavian design and selling goods to the Bristol Guild. He was a senior member of the glass department at the Royal College of Art immediately prior to Sam Herman's arrival there and both wrote about glass and latterly set up the Kings Lynn Glass factory. Important contacts like these, who were also friends, help to explain the presence of different examples of glass in the Collection and why glass has remained very popular at the Guild throughout Ken's career.

Ken's workspace at Park Row.
The desk is by P E Gane from the mid 1930s
and the bird cage by Eleanor Glover, 1996

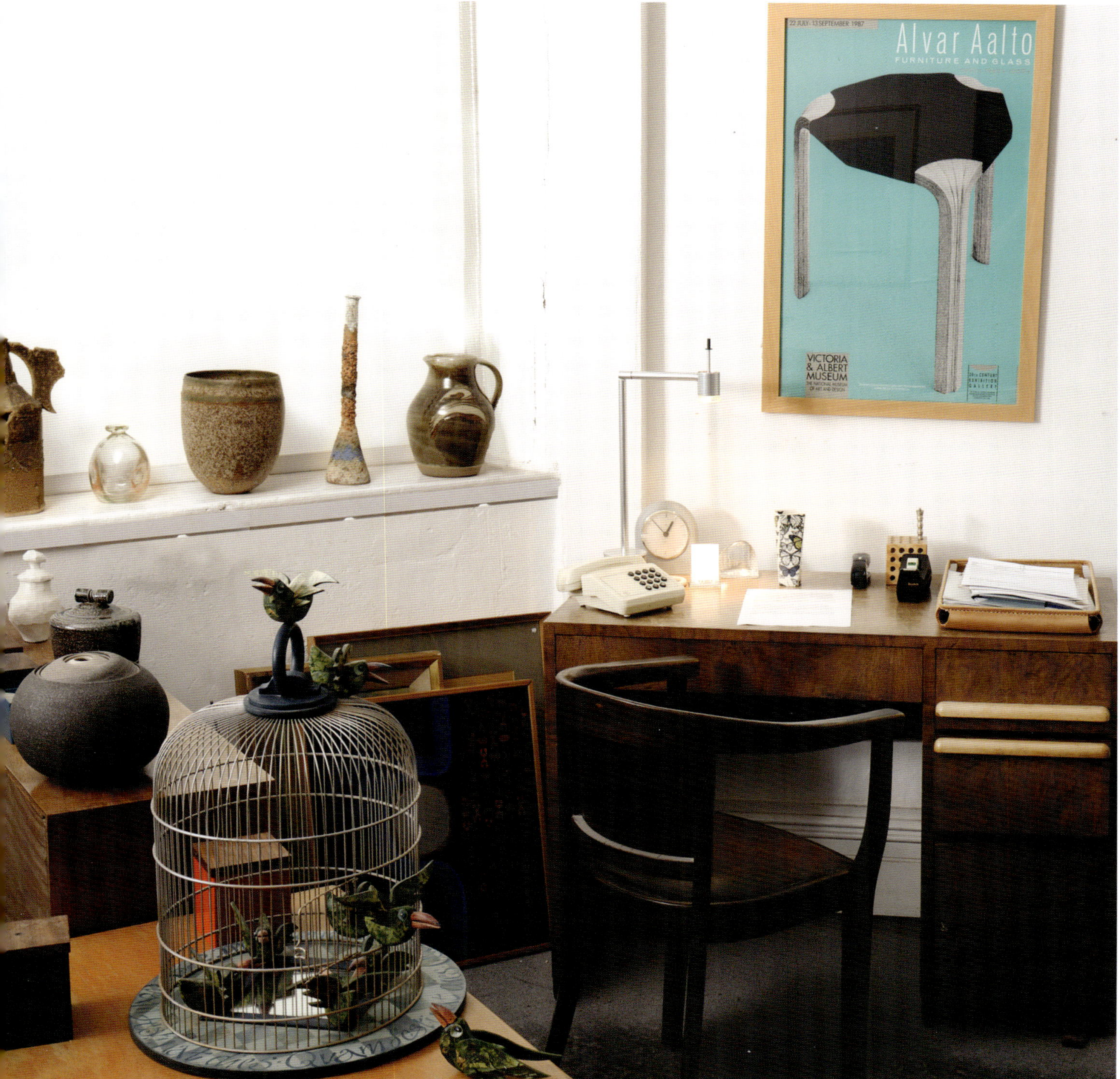
22 JULY - 13 SEPTEMBER 1987
Alvar Aalto
FURNITURE AND GLASS
VICTORIA & ALBERT MUSEUM
THE NATIONAL MUSEUM OF ART AND DESIGN
20th CENTURY EXHIBITION GALLERY

Marcel Breuer and Crofton Gane
THE BAUHAUS in BRISTOL

Ken Stradling is a passionate advocate of good contemporary design and in Bristol follows in the footsteps of another figure with similar ambitions. Crofton Gane lead the Bristol furniture company PE Gane in the years before the second world war and was closely involved with the rise of Modernism in Britain. His work with the Bauhaus furniture designer Marcel Breuer and with other leading figures of the day such as Wells Coates and Jack Pritchard has left a significant legacy. The 1936 Gane Pavilion designed by Breuer for the Royal Agricultural Show in Ashton Park is regarded as one of Modernism's seminal works. Despite the destruction of Gane's factories and showrooms in 1940, he maintained a shop selling good design in Park Street until 1954. Although the collection is primarily modelled around Ken's working career at the Guild, he has also sought out pieces of Gane furniture designed by Marcel Breuer, particularly those originating from Crofton Gane's own house in Westbury Park. These rare and important pieces are a major asset to the collection as a whole. Below, Crofton Gane's great-grandson, design historian Max Gane discusses Breuer and Gane's relationship and its impact.

Oliver Kent

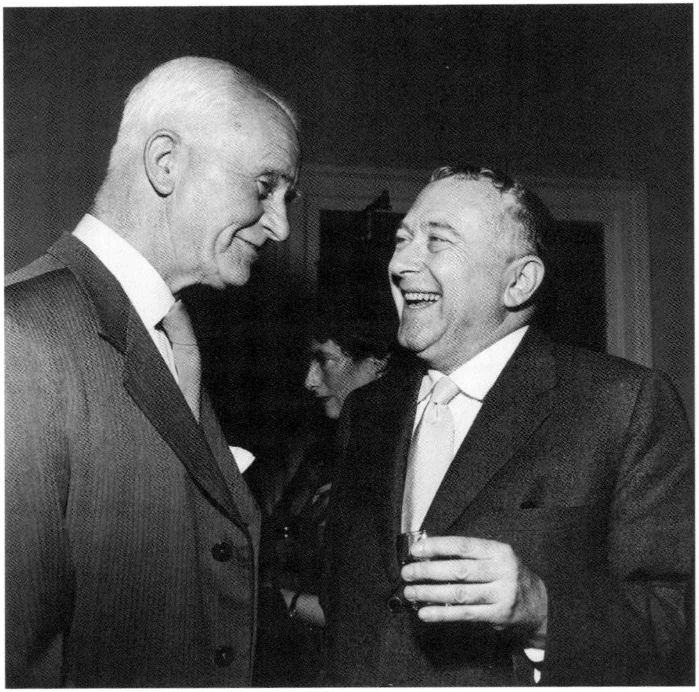

Crofton Gane and Marcel Breuer

'A STYLE TO CALL OUR OWN' – THE GANE LEGACY

Max Gane

In commissioning the Gane Pavilion for the 1936 Royal Agricultural Show in Ashton Court and the refurbishment of his own house in Downs Park West, Bristol, from Marcel Breuer, as well as designs for modernist furniture to be manufactured by the craftsmen in his Bristol factory, Crofton Gane was making a radical departure from the traditions of his company PE Gane's 100-year history.[1]

His progressive attitude was shaped largely after 1919 when he became a member of the Design and Industries Association (DIA). Members of the DIA frequently embarked on field trips all over Europe to see exhibitions and expositions. It was through this that Gane first learned of the new style being developed in Europe. He was particularly influenced when he visited the Paris Exhibition of 1925, where 'he saw at once that a new and vital idea was expressing itself in furniture… and he felt the unmistakable call to introduce it to his own city and the West Country'.[2]

It speaks volumes about Gane's nature that he was able not only to see and understand the importance of the developments taking place in Europe, but that he was willing to risk the prosperity and reputation of his company by asserting that this was the future of the design industry.

His mind made up, Gane set about transforming his showroom in Bristol to a showcase of Modernism. He used his connection with another DIA member, Jack Pritchard, who had established his company Isokon working alongside the architect Wells Coates. When the Bauhaus in Dessau was closed, Breuer's close friend Walter Gropius, the former head, fled to England and was offered work in Pritchard and Coates' company. When Breuer followed two years later, Gropius suggested he design a plywood chair to celebrate the launch of the offshoot company Isokon Furniture, the result being the celebrated Isokon long chair. [3]

1 Gane's furniture business was founded on the ideas underlying the arts and crafts movement in Britain. Originally started by Henry Trapnell in 1824, the company passed to his son Caleb, who was a skilled craftsman trained at the Bristol School of Practical Art. Caleb took on Crofton's father Philip Gane as his business partner and together they expanded the company into Newport and Cardiff, with a five-storey factory in Bristol to supply the three shops.

2 H. W., *A Swan Sings. The House of Gane 1824 to 1954*. London: The Shenval Press, 1954, 18

3 Wilk, C., *Marcel Breuer Furniture and Interiors*. New York: The Museum of Modern Art, 1981, 126-136.

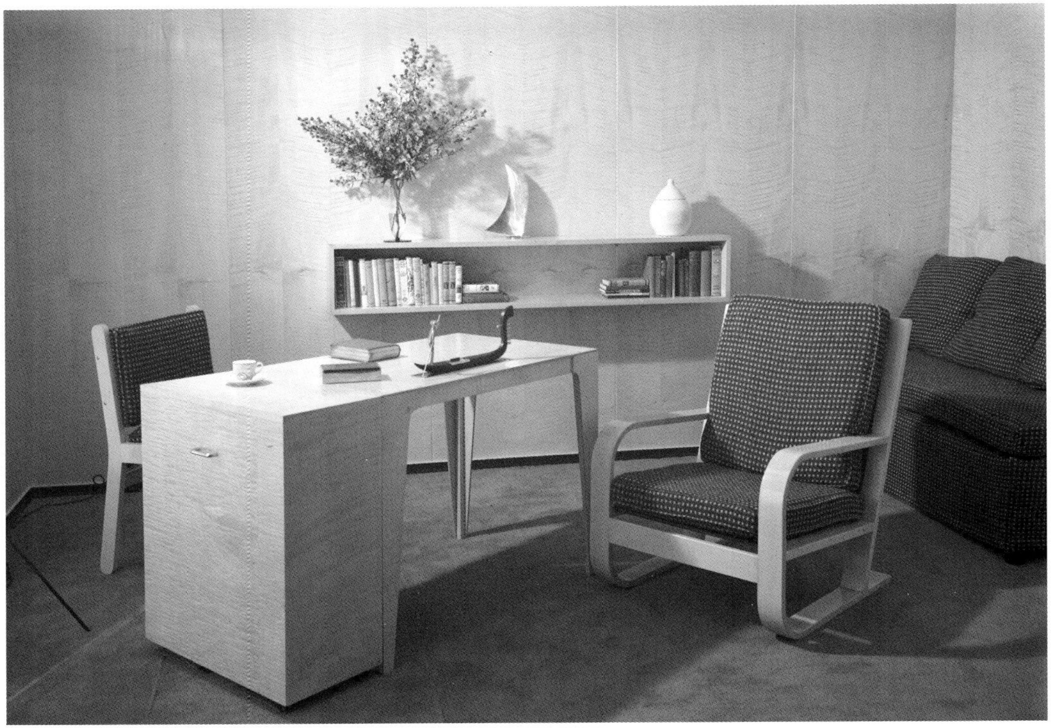

The Drawing room of Crofton Gane's house in 1935 with furniture by Marcel Breuer, made by PE Gane

Gane became a key supplier of the new Isokon furniture and not long after commissioned a unique range by Wells Coates and, of course, the two buildings by Breuer. The decision by Gane to embrace the new style of Modernism was, for his father, quite disturbing. When he entered the transformed showroom for the first time, the expression on his father's face, Crofton recalled, was 'beyond description,' an expression of the fear that only bankruptcy could follow such a major departure from the company's established traditions.[4]

The Gane company's reputation had grown under the guidance of Crofton's father throughout the nineteenth century. At the same time, the Arts and Crafts movement had begun to gather speed, a reaction to the widespread industrialisation then taking place in Britain. The once highly prestigious role of the craftsman was being replaced by the dual

4 H. W., *A Swan Sings. The House of Gane 1824 to 1954.* London: The Shenval Press, 1954, 20-21.

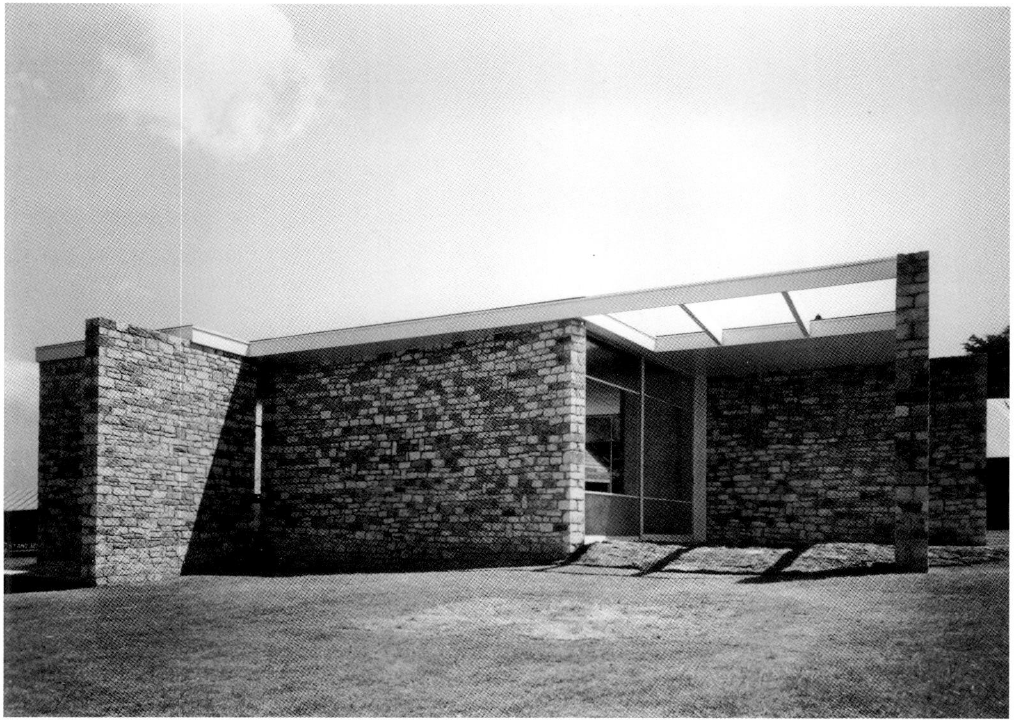

The PE Gane Pavilion designed by Marcel Breuer for the Royal Agricultural Show in Ashton Court in June 1936

roles of designer, independent from the process of making, and a mechanistic team of workers, performing mundane and repetitive tasks as part of a larger assembly line process. The Arts and Crafts movement resisted this division of labour and aimed to reinstate the divine role of the craftsman.

The spirit of the Arts and Crafts movement was very much alive in the day-to-day running of Gane's company. He clearly understood the importance of his craftsmen taking pleasure in their work. He was a model employer, introducing a five-day week, medical care and organising events and excursions.

Far from threatening the livelihood of his craftsmen, Modernism, in Gane's view, embodied a new way of living and a momentous change in society that he was eager to promote. In his newsletter, *News of Gane*, he wrote:

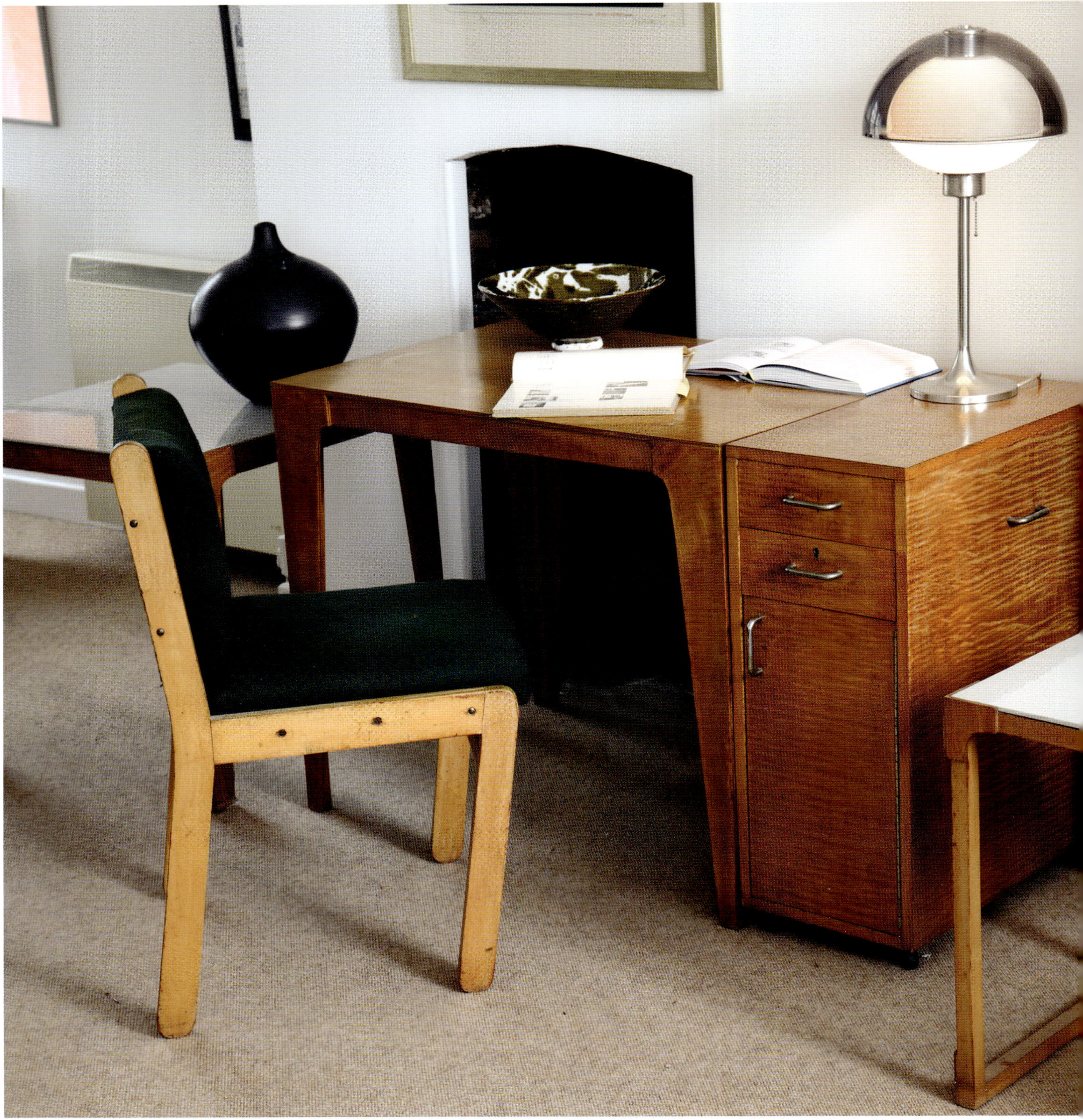

Desk and chair from the Gane House drawing room.
Marcel Breuer for PE Gane 1935 (on loan from Gane Trust)

> For a hundred years, the arts and crafts have been reproducing, reproducing. We have had the Gothic revival and Tudor, Jacobean, Queen Anne and Georgian revivals. Now at last we have a period of out own… It is more than just a new fashion, more than a mere change of taste… We, as craftsmen, are taking part in the birth of a new culture which is a spiritual adjustment to the age in which we live. Perhaps that is why we take pride in our work. It seems to give that work dignity and purpose.[5]

Despite Gane's enthusiasm, the new furniture was received with mixed reactions by the paying customer. Perhaps Gane was ahead of his time. There was a clear divergence between his vision and that of the public to whom he was selling his furniture, reflecting the British public's more conservative attitude to modern design and the promise of a new lifestyle. Not that this deterred Gane; if anything, it would have served only to reaffirm his belief that he could lead the way, and with hindsight it is easy to see that he would have been followed. However in 1940, the College Green showroom was completely destroyed during a sustained air raid on the centre of Bristol. The two workshops soon followed, and despite trading for another 14 years, with no produce to call its own the company finally closed its doors in 1954.[6]

Crofton Gane's commissioning of Marcel Breuer forms a significant part not only of Bristol's history, but the history of modern architecture and design in Britain. The furniture supplied by Gane is emblematic of the shift from the Arts and Crafts into the modern era, and highlights the differences between these two schools of design. However, what Gane achieved was not an exclusive preference of one approach over the other, but a bringing together of the values and ideals which these approaches stood for.

At a time when Britain was reluctant to embrace the machine age, Crofton played an instrumental role in introducing Modernism to the British public. He opened the door to a whole host of design ideas, the influence of which is still being felt today.'

5 Gane, C. *News of Gane*, 2, Nov 1936, 4.

6 H. W., *A Swan Sings. The House of Gane 1824 to 1954.* 1954, London: The Shenval Press, 26.

A CENTRE FOR DESIGN RESEARCH

Oliver Kent / Cleo Witt

> Part of the remit [of the Collection] is to increase knowledge and appreciation of good design.
> Design is everything to me.
> Ken Stradling

In its new home at 48 Park Row the trustees of the Collection are creating a Design Study Centre, a place for visitors to pursue Ken's goal – 'to increase knowledge and appreciation of good design'. It will also be a research resource, with changing exhibitions, public lectures and group visits. There will also be opportunities for volunteering.

Though home to the Ken Stradling Collection, the Study Centre is intended to be more than a museum. It will engage visitors with contemporary design issues, in particular through exhibitions, lectures and collaborative work with similar organisations. The Trust has already contributed to a major exhibition, 'Marcel Breuer in Bristol', at Bristol's Architecture Centre. At Bristol Guild Gallery the trustees curated a retrospective show of work of the ceramic sculptor Dan Arbeid, who died in 2010. Staff and students of Bristol School of Art and Bath Spa University already have access to the Collection.

In creating a charitable trust to care for and show the Collection in a permanent home, Ken and the trustees hope to encourage visitors – students, children, indeed everyone – to understand how design can enhance our lives and thinking. There are objects in the Collection produced by makers working at the very edge of possibility with particular materials and techniques, testing capacities and constraints and solving problems to produce objects that are highly expressive, beautiful and, above all, original. This is what design means and why design history differs from art history. It is also why design is so important as an educational tool, demonstrating 'a strong culture of experimentation, innovation and debate...in a dynamic and vibrant environment that encourages risk and originality [and] diversity in thinking, opinions and ideologies.' (Royal College of Art, School of Design prospectus).

The range of media and production that characterises the Collection is special to it. It is not a collection of ceramics, glass or furniture; it is not a collection of hand-made crafts or factory-made goods; it is all of these things: the product of Ken Stradling's fascination for the *design* process, rather than any single genre, material or technique. Indeed, Ken's interest in

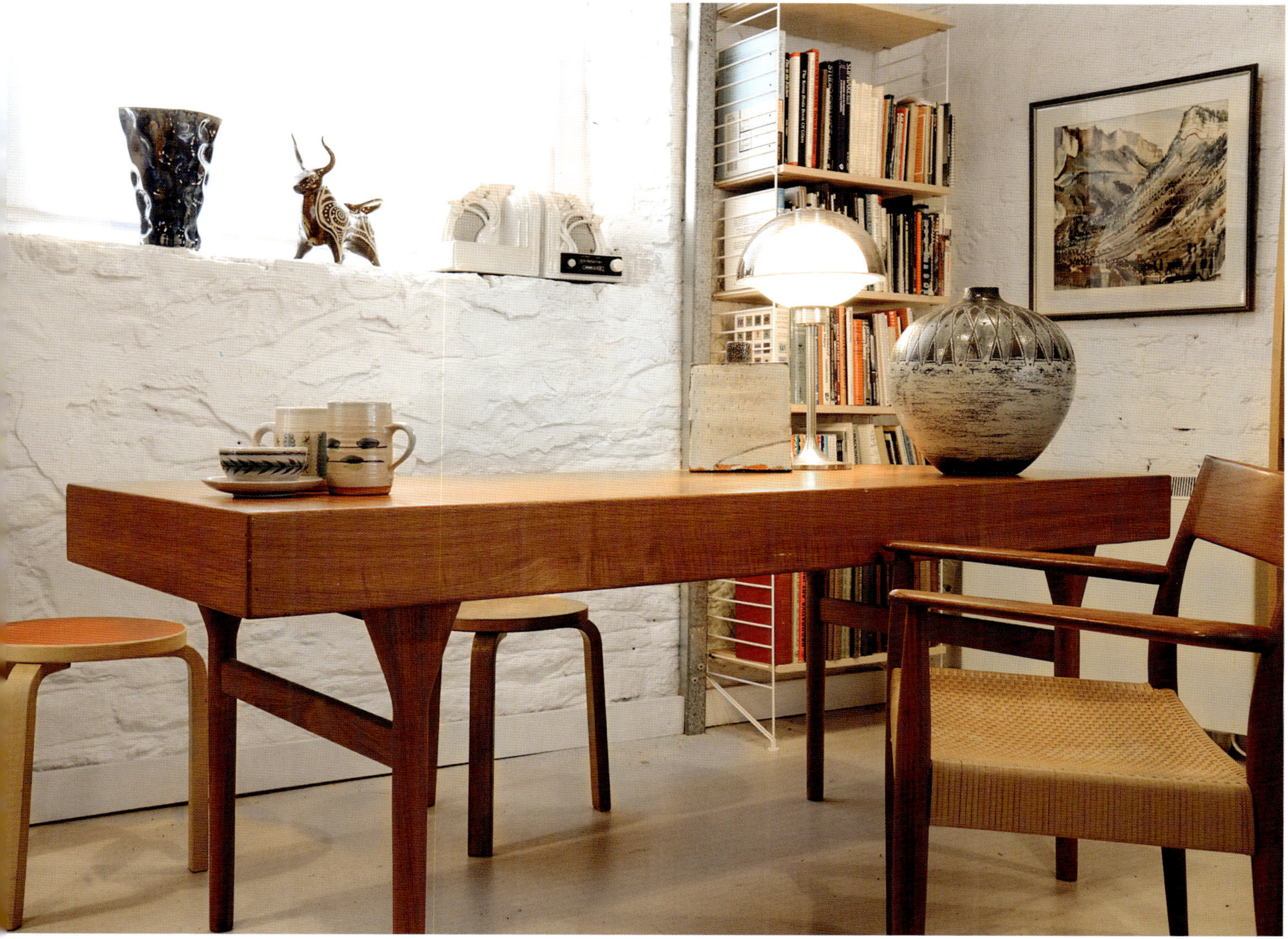

The study area / gallery at 48 Park Row: desk by Nanna Ditzel | domestic ware by Marianne de Trey | large vase by Gustavsberg | chair by Grete Jalk

Student Juliet Hilder from Bristol School of Art studying the collection with trustee Oliver Kent

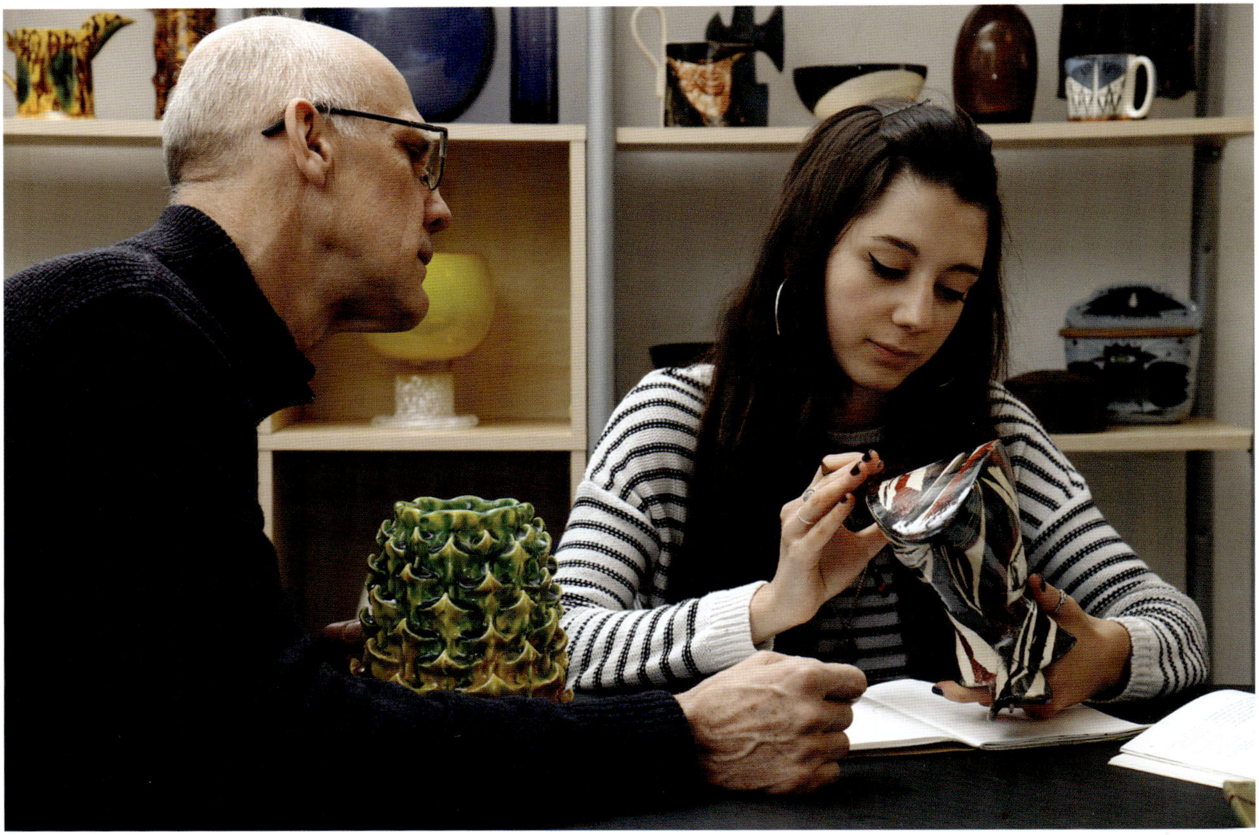

Scandinavian design lies precisely in the knowledge that designers like Nanna Ditzel are able to move freely between furniture, jewellery and textiles.

Some items in the Collection have been acquired for their historical value but most are bought new and reflect the evolving taste and design aesthetic of the second half of the twentieth century and the beginning of the twenty-first. In recent years Ken has added pieces to fill perceived gaps and introduce greater variety in particular areas, but such buying is moderated by personal taste, a subjective view at any one moment of what constitutes good design.

Apart from the individual charm of each object, the Collection as a whole makes powerful cultural statements. Here you can study both objects and archive material to pose questions about recent design history: how did British art glass evolve alongside Scandinavian? What did studio ceramicists learn from mass-produced wares? What was the impact of modernism in the 1930s for British furniture manufacturers? These are national narratives but there is also a compelling local story of post-war Bristol, a city which, in the 1960s and 1970s, cultivated radicalism (reflected for example in the 1963 Bristol Bus Boycott) and community activism. The city has a history of strong and effective community groups: City Docks Ventures, Cyclebag and Sustrans. Ken's involvement as a director at the Dartington Cider Press Centre, and with architects and interior designers, is significant. In the 1930s furniture manufacturer Crofton Gane used his Bristol home to showcase the work of Marcel Breuer and Modernism; in 1965 Ken Stradling worked with the experimental Span Developments at Sneyd Park in Bristol to show contemporary furniture (including work by leading Scandinavian designers) in a modern home.

Underpinning Ken's work at the Guild is a belief in the importance of engaging people in appreciation and critical enjoyment, whether as makers or consumers. A major part of that belief has been in the centrality of the audience. A customer from the 1970s recalls Bristol Guild as:

> 'one of the few places where one knew one would find quality and could expect aesthetic satisfaction. If only there had been more Bristol Guilds and a broader sense of needing to educate the public who knows where we might have landed?'

Ken understands the value to a maker of such an appreciative audience and quotes Roy Strong:

> My call would be for a role for art within education which has far less emphasis on participation and doing and far more on looking and listening or, rather, learning to look and listen for both are highly complex skills. Such a shift in emphasis would also recognise a truth – that few people are destined to become doers in the arts and also that the need for doers is finite. In sharp contrast the real need is for informed patrons and audiences – the demand for them will always be infinite.[1]

As neighbours, it is intended that the Guild and the Study Centre will actively engage audiences with the best of hand-made and commercial design and, by doing so, impart some of the pleasure, understanding and appreciation that Ken Stradling, the incidental collector, has acquired over a lifetime.

---

1 Strong, Roy, *Passions Past and Present.* London 2005, Pimlico.

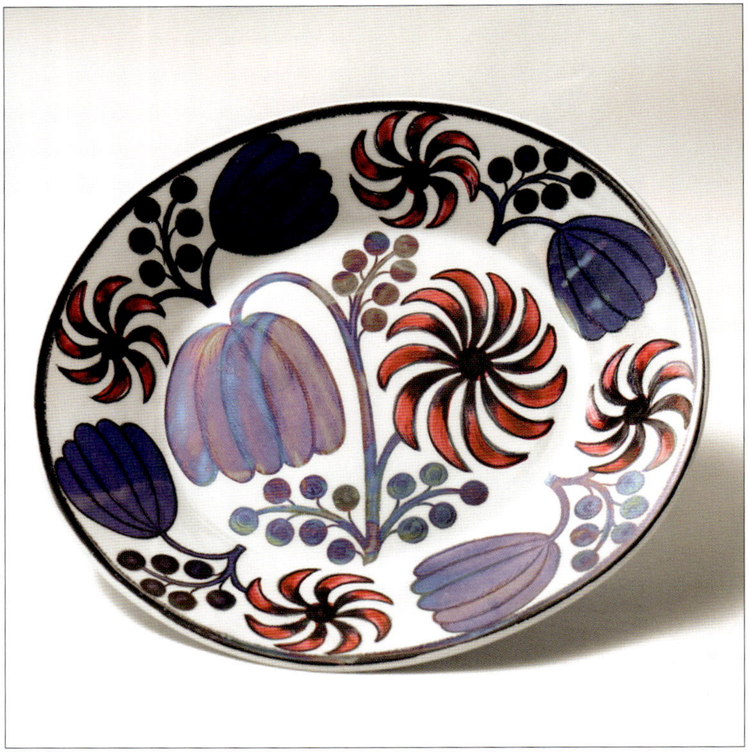

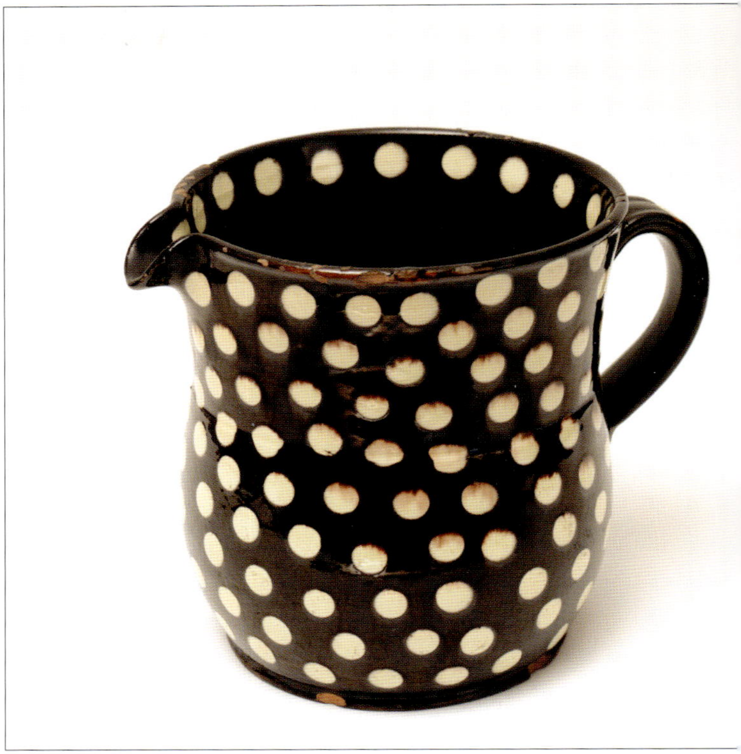

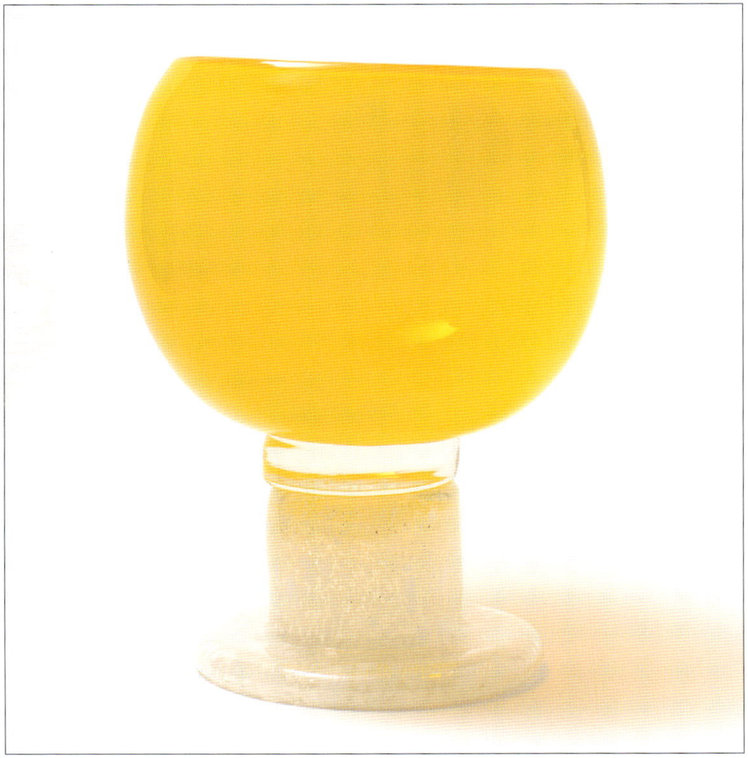

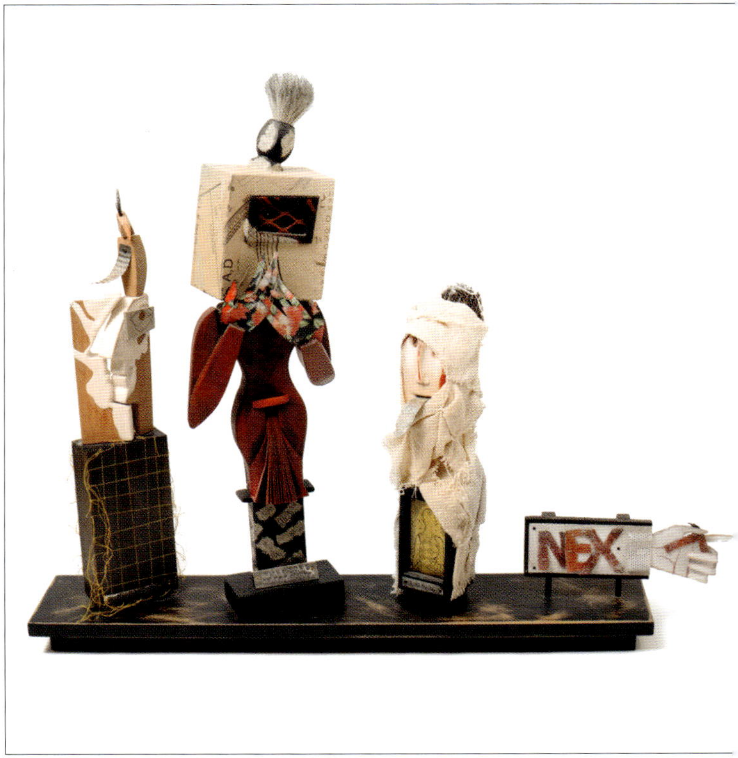
NEX

Contributors

Colin Beales is a retired architect and designer. A close friend of Ken Stradling, he is a trustee of the Ken Stradling Collection.

Max Gane is an architect and writer. He curated the Breuer in Bristol exhibition at the Architecture Centre in Bristol in 2010. He is the great-grandson of Crofton Gane.

Dr Oliver Kent is an art and design historian and potter and teaches at Bristol School of Art. He is a trustee of the Ken Stradling Collection.

Christopher Lloyd is an art historian and former Surveyor of the Queen's Pictures.

Dr Graham McLaren is an art and design historian. He is Head of Design and Critical Studies at Bath School of Art and Design, Bath Spa University.

David Whiting is a writer and critic. He is a trustee of the Anthony Shaw Collection at York Art Gallery.

Cleo Witt is the former Head of Education at the Holburne Museum of Art in Bath. She is a trustee of the Ken Stradling Collection.

Clockwise from top left: dish by Birger Kaipiainen | French provincial slipware jug, early 20th-century | *The Waiting Room*, Eleanor Glover, 2009 | goblet, Kai Franck, Nuutajärvi, 1960s

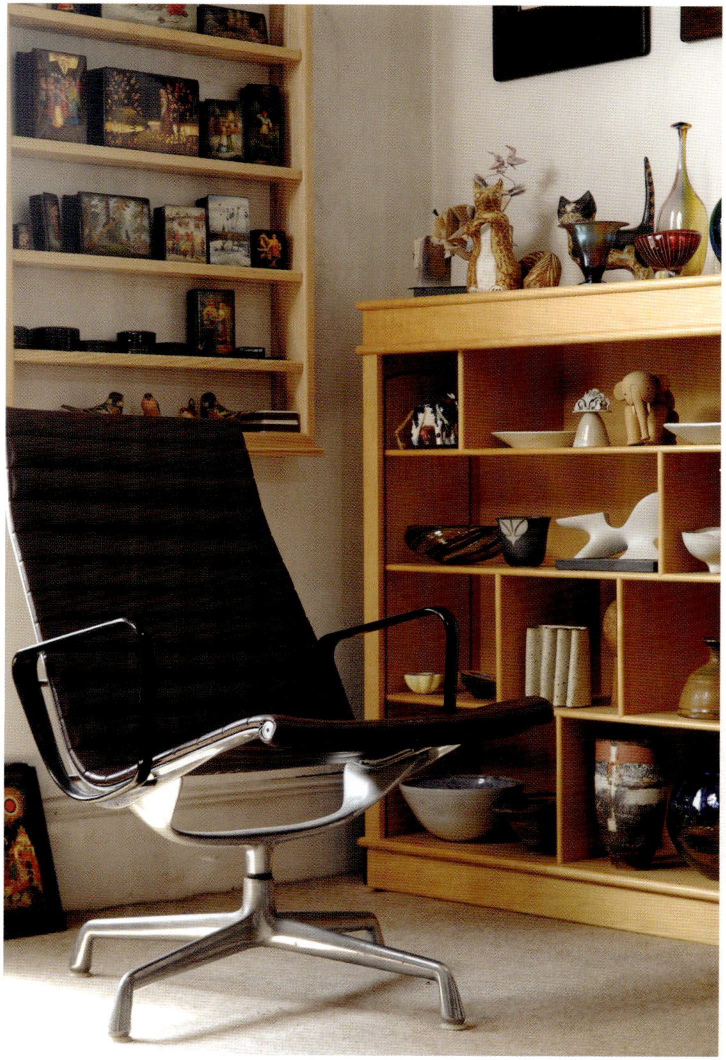

Part of June Lancaster's collection, now incorporated with Ken Stradling's. Eames' *EA Space 116* chair

Bibliography

Anon, 2004, *Bristol Guild 1908-2004*. Bristol: Redcliffe Press.

Gane, Max, 2010, 'A Style to Call Our Own,' *Bristol Review of Books*, 15, 12.

Gane, Max, 2009, 'Breuer in Bristol, Introducing Modernism to Britain in the 1930s,' in Cox, G., Haq, N. and Trevor, T. (eds), *Concept Store #2, Possible, probable and preferable futures*, Bristol: Arnolfini, 79-85.

Kent, O. and Whiting, D., 2011, *Dan Arbeid, 1928/2010, A Retrospective*. Bristol: Ken Stradling Collection.

Morris, S., 2012, 'Bristol Biographies: The Collector,' *Clifton Life*, 144, 52-3.

Sansom, J., 2010, 'Bauhaus Bristol, Marcel Breuer comes to town,' *Bristol Review of Books*, 15, 10-11.

Teuma, Tabitha, 2012, 'Collector's Perspective, Ken Stradling on Marcel Breuer', *Midcentury Modern*, 3, 62-63.

W.H., *A Swan Sings. The House of Gane 1824 to 1954*, London: Shenval Press.

Whiting, D., 2011, 'Dan Arbeid: a rugged beauty', *Bristol Review of Books*, 17, 34.

Interview with Ken Stradling (audio), (12 July 1996). NEVAC 176, 01:01:00. *Recording the Crafts*, School of Creative Arts, University of the West of England, Bristol. www.uwe.ac.uk/sca/research/rtc/index.htm.

Interviews with Ken Stradling (digital video), (1 April 2008). NEVAC 1209, 00:59:26 / NEVAC 1210, 00:56:13. *Recording the Crafts*, School of Creative Arts, University of the West of England, Bristol. www.uwe.ac.uk/sca/research/rtc/index.htm

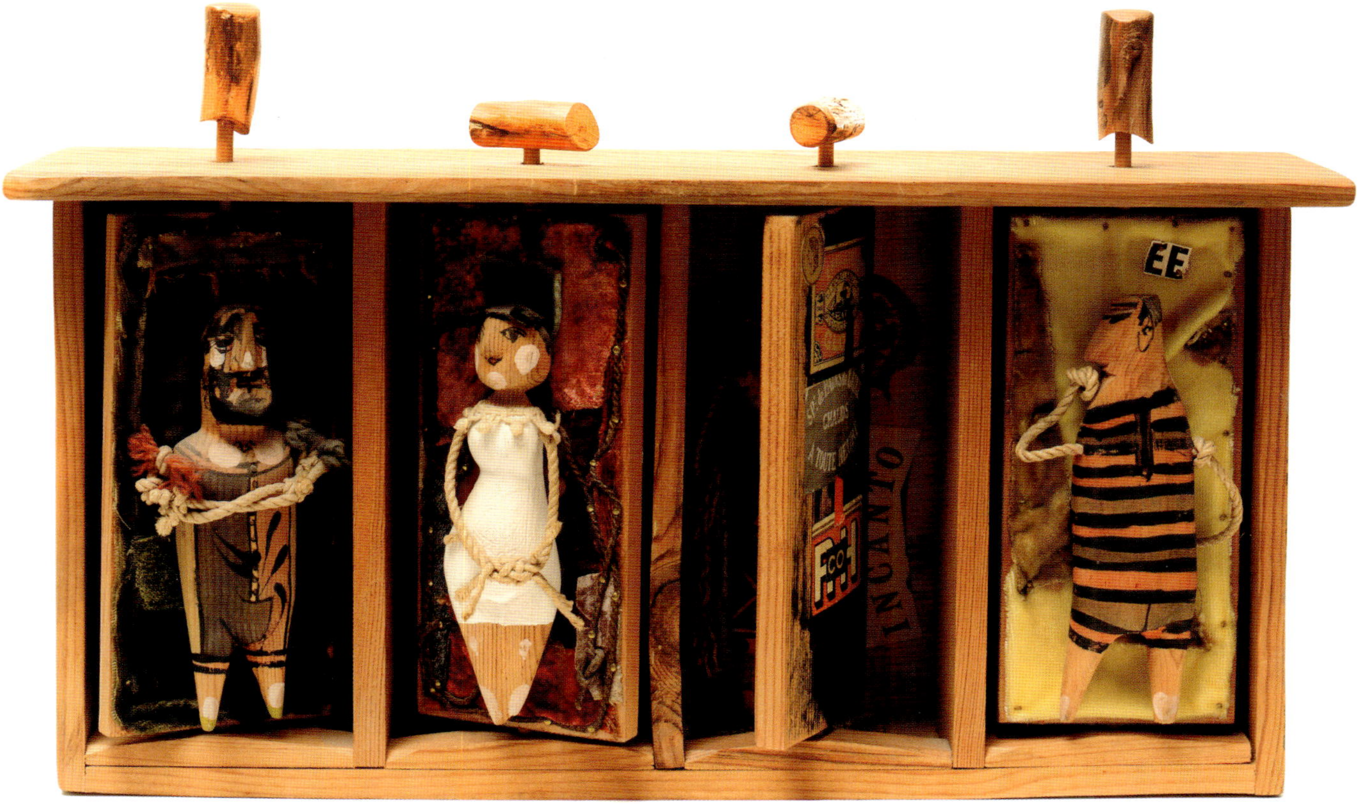

Bathers, Sam Smith, 1961

AFTERWORD

I would like to pay tribute to two people who helped me build this collection:

my wife Betty, an artist who widened my horizon in fine art and introduced me to the new wave of hand-building ceramists of the Central School; and

June Lancaster, my friend and fellow director at the Bristol Guild who travelled with me over many years visiting craftsmen and designers and whose personal collection of some 150 pieces is now incorporated with mine.

Ken Stradling

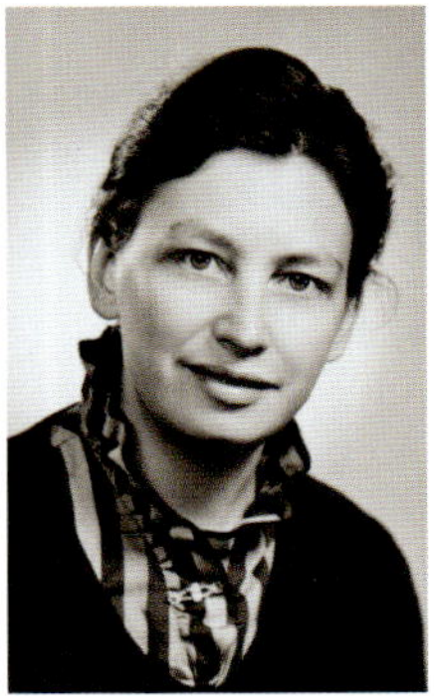

Betty

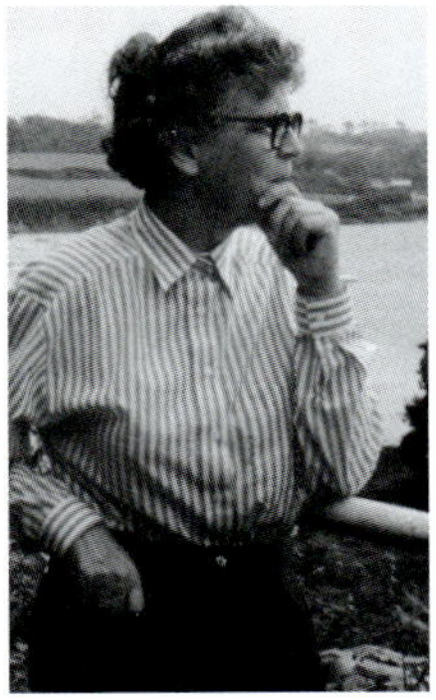

June Lancaster

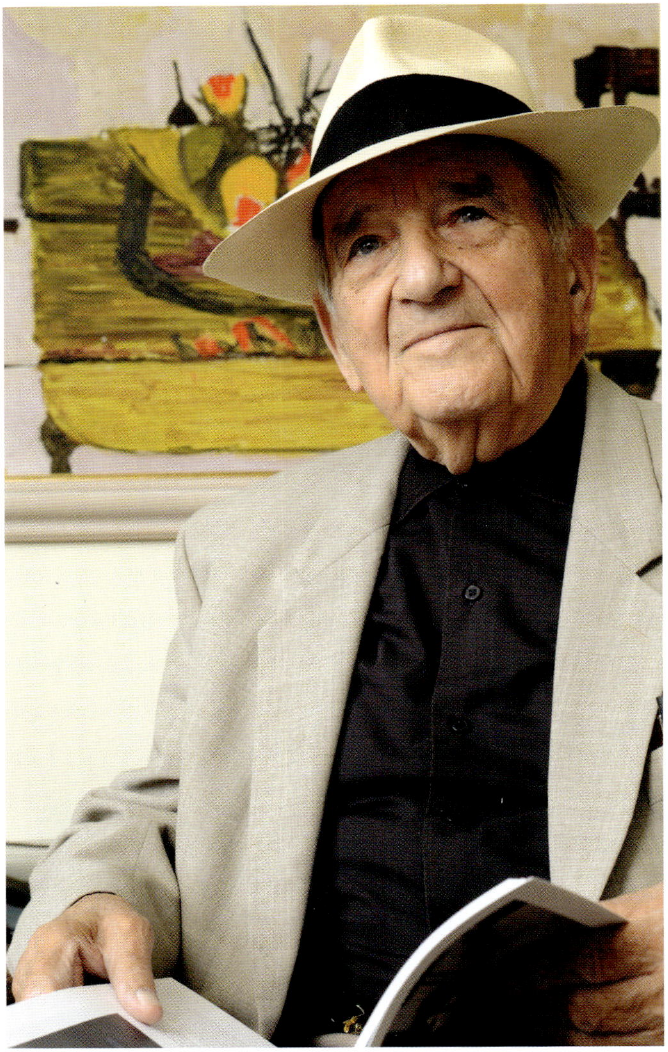

Ken. The painting behind is by Betty Haggar, later Betty Stradling